CONTENTS FAREWELL TO STAR TREK: THE NEXT GENERATION

RODDENBERRY'S VISION

by RICK BERMAN
EXECUTIVE PRODUCER—*STAR TREK: THE NEXT GENERATION*

I knew very little about *Star Trek* when I met Gene Roddenberry, 7½ years ago. But he took me under his wing, so to speak, and I learned a great deal—not only about *Star Trek*—but also about his ideas of what the 24th century will be like.

Gene saw humanity as an evolving species that was going to keep getting better and better. He believed the future was something to look forward to and that the exploration of space and the development of our quality of life were things mankind was going to focus on. His vision of tolerance and cooperation among all beings gave a sense of hope to a lot of people. It also did a good job of entertaining them.

We have been very careful to uphold that attitude. Gene taught me a new language, and now I have become relatively fluent. We've bent his rules a little, but we haven't broken them. *Star Trek: The Next Generation* is not a series about my vision of the future or Patrick Stewart's or anybody else's. It's a series about Gene's vision of the 24th century. As a result, I will continue to follow his rules as long as I'm connected with *Star Trek* in any way.

When *Star Trek: The Next Generation* began in 1987 with the episode "Encounter at Farpoint," it was the beginning of a journey of exploration. The final episode of the series ("All Good Things...") will bring our characters back to that première episode in many respects.

It's going to reintroduce the character of Q, whom we first met on the way to Farpoint Station, and once again ask questions about mankind's position at the threshold of exploration. Hopefully, this final episode will make people stop and think about humanity and what it has in store in the same way the first episode did—but it will do it differently. If anything, that's what *The Next Generation* has come to represent—an opportunity for our audience to think about things in a different way.

It's going to be a wonderful two-hour episode—provocative, full of surprises and one that reflects upon the affection our characters have developed for each other over these seven years. And, above all, it will honor the enduring legacy of Gene Roddenberry. We hope you enjoy it.

GEORGE LANGE/ONYX

DAVID STRICK/ONYX

BERMAN

RODDENBERRY

ON SET

Scheduled for a three-week shoot, the filming of *STNG*'s final episode—the aptly titled "All Good Things..."—began the morning of March 10, 1994. As familiar faces like Denise Crosby, Colm Meaney and John de Lancie took their places alongside regular cast members, veteran director Winrich Kolbe (with Denise Crosby and Michael Dorn, above) got down to business on the bustling set—amid laughter and the occasional tears.

by MICHAEL LOGAN

THE FINAL WEEKS

It's hard to tell what makes Marina Sirtis more upset—the fact that her phenomenal hit series, *The Next Generation*, has been canceled after seven seasons or that none of her six costars seems to be taking it as hard as she is.

"I'm really rather hurt that they're not going to miss me as much as I'm going to miss them," says Sirtis, wiping at her drippy mascara and attempting a droopy smile. Her role as *STNG*'s empath and supershrink Deanna Troi came a few months after the British expatriate landed in Los Angeles. "And I think that's why I'm torn apart. These people—and my husband—are the only family I have in this country. I'm crying just thinking about it."

But, then, this really isn't goodbye.

As Sirtis sits like a lost orphan in the middle of Paramount Studios' cavernous Stage 8, nearby workmen are tearing down the walls of the Sickbay set while sounds of ripping carpet come from the adjacent Transporter Room. In a matter of days, it will all be a misty, water-colored memory. But, simultaneously with the demolition, new sets and new costumes are being created for Sirtis and the rest of the Magnificent Seven—Patrick Stewart, Jonathan Frakes, Brent Spiner, LeVar Burton, Gates McFadden and Michael Dorn—who will next star in the $25-million US motion picture "Star Trek: Generations." If it's the box-office smash Paramount intends it to be, there will be a "Star Trek" feature every 18 to 24 months. There will also be opportunities to guest star on both *Star Trek: Deep Space Nine* and *STNG*'s upcoming replacement series, *Star Trek: Voyager*. And, if they so choose, they can reunite on the sci-fi convention circuit until they're in wheelchairs.

So there will be no official farewell, no last-time-before-an-audience hugfest like the cast of *Cheers* had (nor, merci-

fully, will there be any tacky, drunken revelry on *The Tonight Show*!). Instead, production on the two-hour finale of *STNG*—painfully titled "All Good Things..."—will come to an end in a pretty anticlimactic way. Like each of the show's previous 177 episodes, it will be shot so piecemeal that the last time all seven regulars appear on-camera together—Thursday, March 31— actually occurs five days before the series wraps. (Because production is already two days behind schedule, even the cast party must be thrown before filming has stopped. For details on the party, see the story on page 58.) As a result, "piecemeal" pretty much describes the emotions, too.

"A slight little pang of despair runs through me every time I realize we're going to be on the Bridge or in Picard's quarters for the last time—but there's no real sense of closure," says Rick Berman, executive producer of *STNG* and guardian of the Gene Roddenberry vision. "The movie," he adds, "certainly softens the blow of separation." But nothing softens the bewilderment. No one—from Berman to the Stage 8 custodians—seems to know (or is willing to say) *exactly* why Paramount has photon-torpedoed the most popular and financially lucrative one-hour drama in the history of television syndication.

"There are a lot of reasons why this decision has been made, and I'm not aware of all of them," says Berman, hulking like a giant panda in his production office on the Paramount lot (a plaster bust of Roddenberry sits on his desk—its eyes covered by a red bandanna). "Some of it has to do with Paramount's desire to start a series of motion pictures with these characters— the thinking being that you can't have them in a series *and* in the movies at the same time. The studio also felt it was time to bring on another *Trek* series. There were also certain financial considerations—things I can't go into. But all this was decided two years ago and, with all the changes in Paramount hier-

A BEHIND-THE-SCENES LOOK AT THE FILMING OF THE FINAL EPISODE

John de Lancie and Patrick Stewart receive instructions from director Winrich Kolbe

archy, it's the one thing they've never changed their minds about."

Across the lot in his clutter-filled trailer, Jonathan Frakes (Riker) isn't quite so complaisant.

"If there's any truth to the rumor that our show makes Paramount $80 million US a year, why in God's name do they take off the cash cow?" says Frakes, suddenly breaking his sadness with a Cheshire cat smile. "But they don't ask

MICHAEL WESTMORE —Makeup Design

Most difficult assignment: "Aging everyone 25 years for the finale— creating just the slightest hint of jowl can be a nightmare."

us, do they? One wonders if they are not going to the well one too many times. I hope not. But it's certainly got to be a fear the creators have."

Then again, maybe not. As his towering stand-in steps in for a lighting change, the equally towering Michael Dorn (Worf) grabs a chair in an empty corner of the Ten Forward lounge and offers his point of view:

"There was a different feeling when we first came on board. If there was an answer that you needed, you could always go right to Gene—and the answer made sense. It was all thought out because it was *his* vision. And we're kind of a conglomerate now. We're lost in the machinery." A recurring cast member on *The Mary Tyler Moore Show*, Dorn recalls a much more satisfying sense of completion when the landmark sitcom ended—simply because it did actually end. "We could look back proudly and say *that* and only *that* was *The Mary Tyler Moore Show*. I [tried to share] this feeling with one of the producers—but she was [more inter-

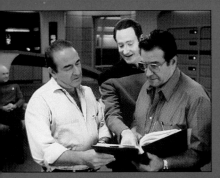

nt Spiner (centre) discusses a fine point
h script supervisor Cosmo Genovese
ht)

Makeup supervisor Michael Westmore
(left) prepares a scene involving a
special effect

ested] in talking about going on to *Star Trek: Voyager*. She's on her way, and I felt like an old shoe. It's sorta like [they're saying], hey, we've got a new group showing up, it's been wonderful, see ya later, have a good finale."

But there are no sore feelings among the crewmates of the USS Enterprise NCC-1701-D.

"We have all the affection in the world for each other," continues Dorn. "I don't know if we're ever going to have this much fun on any future job."

Sirtis seconds that emotion: "For the love and camaraderie to have lasted this long is extraordinary. Everyone behind the camera has said that they've never known actors to get on this well after two years, much less seven." With a raise of an eyebrow and a lowering of voice, she says, "We've *all* heard horror stories about other sets, but we have no horror stories here. Not one." She motions in the direction of the *Deep Space Nine* soundstage. "Even across the street, they're beginning to have horror stories." Now Sirtis is on a roll.

"I don't know if I should tell you this," she giggles, "but we had a director in the first season who did two episodes and then refused to ever come back because the actors were too rowdy. Rick Berman came down to the set, called us all together and literally told us off. He said it was unprecedented in Hollywood that a director would [flee] like that. We were all sitting there like bad 13-year-olds, going, 'Uhhh... sorry, sir'."

Well, did behavior improve?

"Oh, noooooo, it got far worse!" says Sirtis, cracking up. "I dread to think what he'd say if he came back to direct us *now*." But she makes no apologies. "It's kept us together, and it's kept us sane."

The inter-cast dynamics at *STNG* are fascinating to behold—and so is the way the stars lovingly forgive each other's trespasses. Sirtis is the makeup room diva, the one most likely to keep everyone else waiting. Dorn is subject to either extraordinary bouts of charm or extraordinary bouts of angst, while, in

As he did in the pilot episode, "Encounter at Far point," Q places mankind on trial and takes Pica leaping through the past, present and future

contrast, LeVar Burton (Geordi), a Buddhist whose no-frills trailer is at all times wafting with incense, seems to march to a transcendental drummer all his own. A master of the snide understatement, Brent Spiner (Data) is the set's intellect and the cast member whose critical opinion is most highly regarded ("I was thinking of asking him to be my acting coach for upcoming auditions," says Sirtis, "but he'll make me pay"). Then there is the sleek and coltish Gates McFadden (Crusher). Half sophisticate, half earth mama, she has brought her 2-year-old Jack to the set and constantly apologizes for his cranky outbursts—one of which ruins a scene she is playing with Patrick Stewart.

Ahhhh, yes, Mr. Stewart. Even when he's not playing Capt. Jean-Luc Picard, the bald-headed star can't help but stomp about the set like a flat-footed stentorian. He is the ruler of the roost: often funny, often enchanting, and just as often abrupt, moody and manic. It comes as no surprise that Stewart has won international success and numer-

ous trophies for his one-man stage version of "A Christmas Carol"—for he is Ebenezer Scrooge and Tiny Tim all rolled into one. And the cast adores him for it.

But with Stewart self-cast as the enfant terrible, the role of company father figure falls quite naturally to Jonathan Frakes. One is instantly struck by the guy's goodness and decency—a genuine gentleman transported from the age of innocence—and this is further accentuated by the lines and wrinkles in his granddaddy makeup (the STNG finale has Picard quantum leaping between past, present and future, so for several days of the production all characters but Data must be aged 25 years). Sitting on a sunny bench outside the soundstage, "old man" Frakes trades wisecracks with security personnel, happily poses for snapshots with visiting out-of-towners and soaks up every last sweet moment. He is hardly blubbering like Marina Sirtis—but he, too, is a softy.

"This is all very bittersweet...very bittersweet," he says, grasping at his heart.

rf and Tasha Yar,
hey appeared
en years earlier

Miles O'Brien (Colm
Meaney) conferring
with Picard

Q (John de Lancie) at his
taunting best 25 years in the
future

"It's been a very revealing time for us all. I've been very lucky with Riker—he's a good and honorable man. I've always begged for a little more irony, but irony's tough to write. All things being equal, it's been a good lick as they say." And at this time of reminiscence and retrospection, Frakes finds himself thinking about "the people with terminal illnesses whose lives—if we are to believe the letters we get—have been lengthened a little because they so look forward to another episode of our show. They've had miserable hands dealt them, and if they enjoy part of their day because of what we do, then it's a privilege to do it. It's corny to talk about how hopeful Gene's vision of the future is—but it's corny because it's true."

Dorn, who fully admits he's "become quite a cynic," doesn't share Frakes' sentiment: "If I ever thought the *Trek* phenomenon would have a major impact on the way people think and behave, it has since been dashed by all the racism and the killing that we see. If people watched our show and then

went out and applied its messages to their lives, then I'd say we'd done a great thing. But I don't think that's the case."

Still, the incredible hulk does value his opportunities to meet fans one-on-one: "If this show does do anything positive for society, it's that it [features] two black men who are not threatening. Over the years, I've encountered thousands of people at conventions, and I'm very cordial and attentive to everybody. Hopefully they go away with a better understanding of what I and other black people are all about. Because on TV and in the movies, you only see a certain type of black—the gangster or the clown—and that's it."

Things are not so weighty over in the hairdo department, where a gold-encrusted Brent Spiner is having a very unconvincing streak of white painted on to his slicked-back hair. He looks positively skunk-like.

"Unlike the other characters, Data doesn't actually age—though I don't know where they came up with *that*

THE STORY 25 YEARS HENCE: Data has become a professor at Cambridge, whe[re] physicist Stephen Hawking taught in the 20th century; Worf has left Starfleet; Riker, Data, and Picard, who has retired to his family vineyards in France

idea," hoots Spiner as he points out his crow's feet. "If they'd been watching me from the first season, they'd know better!" So why the stripe? "It's a plot point. Data paints it in because he thinks it makes him look more distinguished. [In the future], he's a professor at Cambridge, so it suits his image. But all through the future scenes, the other characters are asking, 'What on earth did you do to your hair?'" The time-trav-

el element poses Spiner with quite a challenge: "I have to play three different Datas—the one we met in the beginning, who had very little understanding of humanity; the Data we know now, who has a much better grasp of the idiosyncrasies and subtleties of humanity; and the Data of the future, who is really, really close to being a human...except for his color."

ROBERT BLACKWELL —Costume Design

Greatest challenge: "Continuity—the finale's future uniforms are designed to look 25 years beyond the new uniforms we haven't even seen yet in Star Trek VII.*"*

THEIR FINAL SCENE

However, an even tougher challenge awaits the entire cast—getting through the very last *STNG* scene that they will ever play together.

On the day of this momentous occasion, the nervous tension is so thick it can only be cut by a machete. All week, the stars have been throwing hissy fits about the ceaseless bombardment of reporters and news crews (so much so that one of the show's harried publicists

...er and Crusher have both become captains of their own ships; Geordi (without his trademark VISOR), Picard, Crusher and Data

asks us not to look the actors directly in the eye). But as the final rehearsal begins, the players gather one by one in Riker's quarters, determined to turn the atmosphere buoyant.

Frakes starts humming the *STNG* theme song. As Brent Spiner joins in, Gates McFadden (wearing curlers the size of frozen juice cans) circles the group with her videocam. Taking a cue, Michael Dorn—in full Worf regalia—pulls out a 35mm camera and also starts documenting. Glancing at her script, Marina Sirtis looks dazed and confused. LeVar Burton hums along with Frakes and Spiner. So, then, does Patrick Stewart. Then Dorn. Then McFadden. Then...it's a free-for-all. As if in a *Star Search* face-off with the Mormon Tabernacle Choir, a glorious chorus of swaying, arm-waving Enterprisers booms out round after round, interrupted only by the plaintive cry of Marina Sirtis. "Why are everybody else's script pages yellow when mine are cherry?" asks the tear-streaked beauty. Michael Dorn pretends to sob.

"Since this is our last day, there's something I've been meaning to tell you all," says Patrick Stewart, as he puts his arm romantically around a big, moustachioed stagehand. Frakes laughs. So does Dorn. So does Burton. Another chorus of the *STNG* theme begins. It is almost immediately interrupted by finale director Winrich Kolbe. It's time to get serious.

Sirtis (who finally has her updated yellow pages in hand) rehearses her lines in a goofy cockney accent. McFadden—as if saving herself for the camera—delivers hers in monotone. The boys giggle through theirs—all except Spiner, who is the only one trying to achieve any semblance of character. The energy is almost combustible. Frakes flubs a line. The actors backtrack in the script a bit, but when Frakes gets to his line he flubs it again. Patiently, they backtrack once more. When he flubs it for the third time, all six of his comrades stare at him in disbelief.

"Well, what are they gonna do," shrugs Frakes, "FIRE ME???!!!"

CAST PROFILES

by MICHAEL LOGAN

PATRICK STEWART

After years of acclaimed performances with the Royal Shakespeare Company and the BBC, Patrick Stewart went to America to try his luck with *STNG*—and he was so sure a mistake had been made that he didn't unpack his suitcase for six weeks. "[The producers had] an option on my contract after the pilot," Stewart recalls, "and I had a feeling they would probably [decide] that maybe they could do better elsewhere. So I was well prepared to be given the arm-around-the-shoulder treatment...but it never came about."

The seven-year personal evolution of Capt. Jean-Luc Picard is of particular pride to Stewart: "He has become considerably more relaxed, more light-hearted, more humorous, more generous and altogether more adventurous. He is also much more comfortable around the crew. One of the features of this series has been the extent to which Picard defers. It's now a natural part of the process: He always listens, he will always ask questions and hear opinions."

"From time to time, I've heard that what they call Picard's 'command style' has become textbook material in all sorts of institutions and establishments where this kind of thing is taught. A civil pilot recently told me that when [he

went back for his] reexamination, they actually demonstrated Picard's Bridge style as the ideal that should be aimed for—the proper use of authority, being aware of being part of a team, and so on. And that's quite flattering."

Each of the five *STNG* episodes Stewart directed holds a very warm spot in his heart. But, he admits, "if I were playing the desert island game—what one episode would you take with you?—it would be 'The Offspring,' one of the best stories we've ever told. It had a breathtaking leading performance from Brent Spiner and a dazzling supporting performance from Hallie Todd, who played the android child Data created. It also happened to be Jonathan

Frakes' first show as a director. [He] paved the way for others of us to direct."

Frakes also gave Stewart his most memorable laugh. "In [an episode in] the first season, there was some crisis in engineering, and Jonathan had one line: 'It wasn't him, it never was. It was his assistant.' And he simply couldn't say it. And the hysteria spread like brush fire. It brought the set to a halt for about 45 minutes." But Stewart, who has previously discussed his abusive childhood with the press, says, "The individual laughs are simply overwhelmed for me by the memory of unending, unbroken laughter on this show for seven years. I made up for all the laughter I never had during the previous 47 by the amount of laughing I've done since I joined this show."

CHARACTER BIO

CAPT. JEAN-LUC PICARD

2305: Born to Maurice Picard and Yvette Gessard in LaBarre, France

2323: Accepted at Starfleet Academy; only freshman ever to win Academy Marathon (40K run on Danula II)

2326: Looses his heart, replaced surgically by an artifical one, in a bar fight with a Nausicaan

2327: Graduates class valedictorian

2333: Assumes command of the USS Stargazer—at 28, one of the youngest Starfleet captains

2354: Picard's best friend, Jack Crusher, dies under his command; in the Battle of Maxia against the Ferengi, Picard executes the Picard Manoeuvre making his starship appear to be in two places at once

2363: Assumes command of the USS Enterprise NCC-1701-D

PERSONAL BIO

Birthday: July 13; born in Mirfield, England
Family: Divorced, with two grown children

TELEVISION
- *I, Claudius*
- *Smiley's People*
- *Tinker, Tailor, Soldier, Spy*
- *Death Train*
- *Saturday Night Live*

FILMS
- "Hedda"
- "Excalibur"
- "Lifeforce"
- "Lady Jane"
- "Gunman"
- "Robin Hood: Men in Tights"
- "The Pagemaster"

STAGE
- "Who's Afraid of Virginia Woolf?"
- "Anthony and Cleopatra"
- "A Chrismas Carol"

DIRECTOR—STAGE
- "Every Good Boy Deserves Favour"

DIRECTOR—*STNG*
- "In Theory"
- "Hero Worship"
- "A Fistful of Datas"
- "Phantasms"
- "The Good Fight"

JONATHAN FRAKES

"There are far worse fates than being permanently identified with the legend that is *Star Trek*," says Jonathan Frakes. "I'll take a career like William Shatner's or Leonard Nimoy's any time." And like those two space cowboys before him, Cmdr. Riker frets not about future typecasting. Instead, he's determined to turn *Trek* stardom into future security: Since Season 3, Frakes has been directing select episodes of *Next Generation* and next hopes to "cash in some chips at Paramount so they'll let me direct *Deep Space Nine* and their new series *Voyager*. Like every other director in town, I'd love to do *NYPD Blue* and *Law & Order*. And I've also optioned a couple of movie scripts I want to direct. I'd like to sell them to USA or TNT or..." He pauses and then laughs, "...or whoever will buy them."

Not that he plans to give up acting. Frakes, who was recently seen in the poorly received *North and South* sequel "Heaven and Hell" ("I had a very small part, so I don't feel too bad, or too guilty"), says he'd commit to another quality series "in a heartbeat—especially if it was a sitcom. Hey, I was around and struggling long before *The Next Generation* came

along. I don't have to be kicked in the head to recognize a good job. In fact, for most of the cast, the timing for this show couldn't have been better. We were all far more experienced at *not* working."

And like most of his costars, Frakes has contributed creatively throughout *STNG*'s seven-year run. "The producers probably feel we've been a pain in the neck, but all we've ever wanted was to maintain the level of integrity that Gene Roddenberry created. I'm sure they'd say we've had more input than we deserved and we feel we've had less than we deserved, but in general they've been very receptive." Frakes, a real-life jazz freak, says his favorite episode (in addition to "The Offspring," his first directing effort) is probably "11001001," which stemmed from a brainstorming session between Frakes and Maurice Hurley, one of *STNG*'s original producers. In it, "the crew went on to the holodeck and turned it into New Orleans, and I played trombone with the band. It was great fun. Later, an interest in jazz became part of Riker's character."

He smarts at *STNG*'s year-in, year-out Emmy brushoff: "I think it's an insult to Brent Spiner and Patrick Stewart. They have done work on this show that is as good as anything I've ever seen on television. But personally? It doesn't bother me." But then Frakes has his own little trophy on the way: He and wife Genie Francis (*General Hospital*'s Laura) are expecting their first baby in August.

"For a surprise, it couldn't have been better timing," giggles Frakes. "I am told the biggest change and the hardest job of my life is about to begin—and I'm so excited I'm [bursting]. In a way, it has made the finality of this show a little less painful for me. I have something far more important going on."

PERSONAL BIO

Birthday: Aug. 19 (same as Gene Roddenberry)
Family: Married to Genie Francis (*General Hospital*)
Academic: Penn State, Harvard, Loeb Drama Center

TELEVISION
- *Falcon Crest*
  —recurring role
- "Bare Essence"
- "Paper Dolls"
- *The Doctors*
- "Dream West"
- *North & South I, II, III*

DIRECTOR—*STNG*
- "The Offspring"
- "Reunion"
- "The Drumhead"
- "Cause and Effect"
- "The Quality of Life"
- "The Chase"
- "Attached"
- "Sub Rosa"

CHARACTER BIO

CMDR. WILLIAM T. RIKER

2335: Born in Valez, Alaska, to Kyle Riker, a Starfleet civilian adviser, and his wife, who died when Will was 2
2350: Abandoned by his father, estranged until 2365
2353: Enters Starfleet Academy
2364: Declines command of USS Drake; assigned to the USS Enterprise, as executive officer. Prior service: USS Pegasus, USS Potemkin, USS Hood. First Starfleet officer to serve aboard a Klingon ship, the Pagh. Declines command of the USS Aries, and USS Melbourne.
2369: Meets his double, William Thomas, created eight years earlier by a transporter beam malfunction

BRENT SPINER

"My biggest fear about Data was that he would be an incredibly limiting experience—he seemed a very small palette on which to paint," says Brent Spiner, who was cast as the starship's emotionless android after spending several versatile years on and off-Broadway. But Spiner quickly found out otherwise—in the second episode, to be exact—when the Enterprise crew caught a virus and took on personalities unlike their own. "'The Naked Now' wasn't a well-loved episode, because the audience didn't know our characters well enough to see us doing anything alternative—but I was called upon to do more schtik than I ever imagined I'd be doing. Then, in the first season, we were playing gangsters in a 1940s Dixon Hill mystery. And since then I've played a minimum of 20 different characters on the show—we've done Westerns, the Three Musketeers, Sherlock Holmes, Henry V, Prospero. Data's been possessed by other creatures at least 10 times. I've played his evil brother and his father. He turned out to be as unlimiting a character as I could ever hope to play."

Like Spock, who came before him, and Odo, who came after him, the oddball Data instantly emerged as the audience favorite—a compliment that Spiner modestly brushes aside. "I think he's appealing to a lot of people who [consider themselves] outsiders. Initially, Gene conceived Data to be a one-man Greek chorus—a sweet, innocent creature, incapable of cruelty, who reflected on humanity from an outsider's point of view. But he's a productive outsider. He's still a superhero, an incredible brain and a friend to everyone on the ship. Though he is alienated by his lack of emotion, he is not paralyzed by it. And that's a very strong statement."

So what's Spiner going to do next? "If the history of hit TV shows tells us anything," he heartily laughs, "I'll most likely be on the first train to has-been city—and that's just a quick stop on the way to oblivion. Who knows? At this point, it's anybody's guess what's going to happen. The beauty of the character is that I've been in a very high profile and, thanks to the gold mask, anonymous all at the same time. But there's no getting around it—for the rest of my life, I'm Data. I would love to think the audience will instantly accept me as another character. But in reality, the very best I can hope for is that the audience will see me in future parts and say, 'Oh my God, that's Data!' and then forget about it 10 minutes later."

Not unlike his character, Spiner says he feels very little about the show's cancellation. "Maybe six months from now it'll hit me that I'm really sad. And if I have another job by then," he says with a sly smile, "I won't think about it at all!" Still, he has no expectation of finding greater success. "*Star Trek* is incomparable to any other phenomenon. Tarzan had his day. James Bond had his. But I'll never do anything bigger than this—because there *isn't* anything bigger."

PERSONAL BIO

Birthday: Feb. 2; born in Houston, Texas
Famly: Single
Academic: Attended the University of Houston

STAGE
- "Every Good Boy Deserves Favour"
- "The Seagull"
- "Sunday in the Park With George"
- "The Three Musketeers"
- "Big River"
- "Little Shop of Horrors"

FILMS
- "The Miss Firecracker Contest"
- "Stardust Memories"

TELEVISION
- *Cheers*
- *The Twilight Zone*
- *Night Court*
- *Hill Street Blues*

MUSIC
- Released album "Ol' Yellow Eyes Is Back," background vocals by the Sunspots (Stewart, Frakes, Burton, Dorn)

CHARACTER BIO

LT.-CMDR. DATA

2336: Second android created by Dr. Noonien Soong on Omicron Theta; deactivated by Soong prior to the Crystalline Entity's attack on the planet

2338: Discoved by the crew of the USS Tripoli

2341: Enters Starfleet Academy

2364: Assigned to USS Enterprise; meets his android brother, Lore

2366: Creates an android child, naming her Lal, who dies because of a malfunction

2367: Meets his father, Dr. Noonian Soong

2369: Accidentally sent back to 1893 San Francisco, where he meets Guinan

2370: Meets his android mother, Juliana Tainer

GATES McFADDEN

Though Gates McFadden's run on *The Next Generation* was shorter than that of her costars (her character—Chief Medical Officer Beverly Crusher—was written out for Season 2), she more than made up for it with her dialing finger. "Just ask any of the producers," says McFadden, flashing a naughty grin. "Over the years I was *always* making phone calls to say, 'Gee, couldn't we make Crusher a little stronger on page 23?' or 'All the men get to say things in the last scene—what happened to the women?' Of course, some things you win and some things you lose." But mostly, McFadden —and the fans—have triumphed.

"I was very disturbed—as were many viewers who wrote in—when Crusher's [romantic] relationship with Picard seemed to disappear. It was as if it had never existed. In fact, I was hired to play his love interest—that's what it even said in the job description. Had she just been a doctor and a mother, I would not have taken the job. I wanted [Crusher] to have range." McFadden credits *STNG*'s sole female producer, Jeri Taylor, with eventually getting the relationship back on track.

The recent episode "Journey's End"— featuring a return appearance by Wil Wheaton as Beverly's son, Wesley— also addressed one of McFadden's long-

time concerns. "When I returned in the third season, I felt the relationship between mother and son was being given very short shrift. Whenever Wesley needed any wisdom or a mentor, he always went to one of the male figures on the ship. I thought, hmmmm, that's funny. Here we are in the 24th century with a single parent who's the equivalent of Surgeon General of the galaxy, and it seems sort of strange that [our relationship] only consists of my making peanut butter sandwiches. Of course, you always want to have that side—it's a wonderful side—but there was so much more to explore." Any possibility of that was cut short when Wheaton departed the series, in Season 4, but after some tender rebonding in "Journey's End" (as Wesley got Mom's support on his resignation from Starfleet), McFadden happily concedes "the relationship is now greatly improved."

And, yes, there *is* life after *The Next Generation*—with McFadden the first to prove it. Even before the series finale was in the can, the actress was jetting back and forth to Portland, Ore., to film a juicy ABC pilot called "Mystery Dance." A whodunit comedy borrowed freely from the movie "Manhattan Murder Mystery," it features Peter Riegert and Jane Curtin in the Woody Allen/Diane Keaton roles, while McFadden (as Curtin's wisecracking buddy) steps into the shoes previously filled by Alan Alda. If it gets picked up, she'd happily jump right back into the series grind.

"And besides," says McFadden with glee, "I'd get to be sarcastic—which we were *never* allowed to be on the Enterprise."

CHARACTER BIO

DR. BEVERLY CRUSHER

2324: Born to Paul and Isabel Howard in Copernicus City, Luna
2342: Enters the Starfleet Academy medical school
2348: Marries Lieut. Jack Crusher
2349: Gives birth to son Wesley
2350: Obtains her medical degree
2352: Serves her residency on Delos IV under Dr. Dalen Quaice
2354: Widowed when husband Jack, assigned to USS Stargazer, dies on Away Team mission under the command of Capt. Picard
2364: Assigned to USS Enterprise as Chief Medical Officer
2365: Accepts position as head of Starfleet Medical
2366: Rejoins the Enterprise as Chief Medical Officer
2370: Inherits the family ghost

PERSONAL BIO

Birthday: Aug. 28; raised in Ohio
Family: Son, James Cleveland McFadden Talbot, 2
Academic: B.A., Brandeis University; faculty member at NYU Graduate School, Brandeis University, and University of Pittsburgh

TELEVISION
- *Dream On*
  —guest star
- Beyond the Groove

FILMS
- "The Muppets Take Manhattan"
- "Labyrinth"
  —director of choreography and puppet movement
- "Taking Care of Business"
- "The Hunt for Red October"

STAGE
- "To Gillian on Her 37th Birthday"
- "How to Say Goodbye"
- "Cloud 9"
- "Emerald City"
- "L'Histoire du Soldat"
- "Every Good Boy Deserves Favour"
- "Carnival des Animaux"
  —narrator
- "Viva Detroit"

DIRECTOR—*STNG*
- "Genesis"

MARINA SIRTIS

When Marina Sirtis said goodbye to her native England in 1986 to try her luck in Hollywood, she sobbed so much on the flight over that the captain —in an effort to cheer her up—invited her to visit the cockpit to watch him fly the plane.

"I was simply miserable," recalls Sirtis, "but I didn't want to be one of those people who turn 50 and say, "If only I'd gone to the States, life would have been different. The moment I got to Los Angeles, I knew I was home." The show-biz wannabe took work folding sweaters at the Beverly Center shopping mall until she was called to audition for Deanna Troi, *STNG*'s half-human, half-Betazoid psychologist—a role that has occasionally been frustrating.

"Don't get me wrong," says Sirtis. "I am *very* appreciative of every storyline Troi got, especially because I am not one of the Big Three. But [I felt] a kind of disappointment that so many were "love" episodes. The stories that stand out in my mind aren't the girlie ones. I loved 'Power Play,' where Troi's body was inhabited by a man, and 'Face of the Enemy,' where she was abducted by the Romulans—but abducted because she was an empath, not because she was a woman." Sirtis acknowledges that the *STNG* writers "have been handicapped by the fact that both of our women—Troi and Crusher—are in caretaking professions. That's why I was sad when Denise Crosby (Tasha Yar) left the show. As security chief, she was doing a man's job—if you want to put it in sexist terms—and when we lost her we lost a lot. I think they've learned their lesson and addressed [the problem] on *Deep Space Nine.*"

Still, Sirtis concedes there has been some "progression" in *STNG*'s image of women over these seven years. "I feel we could have gone further with the storylines, but the television audience wants glamor and action and escapism—and you have to abide by those rules. We may be doing a show based in a 24th century where, as Gene Roddenberry envisioned, we will have evolved upwards into a higher form of being. But our show is still being watched by 20th-century males."

Though Sirtis loves playing the convention circuit, you won't catch her "doing" Troi on stage. "The fans get really upset," she admits, "but they understand when I explain my concern about getting too associated with my character in the public eye. In England—where I've played everything from Ophelia in 'Hamlet' to Magenta in 'The Rocky Horror Show'—you don't get typecast. But here it is a problem and a worry." While she's OK about the occasional *STNG* movie, Sirtis says she'd turn down any offer to take Troi to *DS9* or *Voyager* for a guest stint. "But," she hints broadly, "I'd be interested in doing guest spots as *another* character."

Her only regret? "That I could never make Troi funny. After seeing me at the conventions, people will say, 'Gosh, you're so funny—you should do comedy.' But Troi has no timing. None! Every time she's tried to do a gag, it just goes flat. I've actually spoken to psychologists about it."

CHARACTER BIO

COUNSELOR DEANNA TROI

2336: Born to Betazoid Lwaxana Troi and human Ian Andrew Troi, a Starfleet officer; later studies psychology at the University of Betazed and meets Will Riker

2364: Assigned to the post of ship's counselor on the USS Enterprise NCC-1701-D

2365: Gives birth to an alien child, naming him Ian Andrew after her father

2369: Revived from the dead by Dr. Crusher; kidnapped by the Romulan underground, serves undercover as Maj. Rakal of the Tal Shiar (Romulan Intelligence)

2370: Learns of her older sister, Kestra, who died accidentally shortly after Deanna's birth; passes the Bridge Officer's test

PERSONAL BIO

Birthday: March 29; born in London, England
Family: Married to Michael Lamper
Academic: Guild Hall School of Music and Drama, Worthing Repertory Theatre

TELEVISION
- "One Last Chance"
- "Beyond the Groove"

STAGE
- "Rocky Horror Show" (Europe)

FILMS
- "The Wicked Lady"
- "Waxwork II: Adventures in Time"
- "Death Wish 3"
- "Deadly Seduction"

MICHAEL DORN

"Emotionally, I really haven't come to grips with the end of the series yet," says Michael Dorn. "But I *do* know one thing: I'm gonna be glad to get out of this makeup!" On each of his work days since the 1987 debut of *Star Trek: The Next Generation*, Dorn has undergone a 90-minute hair and latex transformation to become Worf, the Starfleet Klingon whose beastly exterior belies a beautiful soul. And that very duality is Dorn's proudest accomplishment.

"Gene Roddenberry gave me great creative leeway, and as a result I feel I've been the architect for all Klingons. Initially, the *Trek* audience perceived them as wild, ambitious and murderous—but, as Worf developed over the years, we've seen that they are loving, thoughtful, honor-bound and almost Shakespearean in their eloquence." His most memorable episode? Well, Dorn is torn. "Every year, there's a new one I'm proudest of. 'Heart of Glory,' in which we first discovered that Worf knows he's a true Klingon, was an important one for me." So were the episodes in which Worf dated and mated with K'Ehleyr (played by *Love & War*'s Suzie Plakson) and the ones where he dealt—not very well, mind you—with his wayward offspring, Alexander (played by Brian Bonsall).

"But my crowning glory," says Dorn, "has been the relationship between Worf and Troi. It's not consummated in the series finale, but we do put a sort of button on the whole thing. We leave you knowing there's *something* there."

Reflecting on the upside and downside of *Trek*'s success, Dorn admits he's enjoyed "the freedom that comes from not having to worry about every penny. But you also start to accumulate...stuff. And eventually you wind up with too much stuff. I mean, I own a pinball machine! I've now developed such an aversion to material things that I just want to unload—get rid of the house and the possessions and get a little apartment somewhere. It can become a real trap." And on the subject of tangibles, Dorn has never been wild about those *Next Generation* action figures. "It's just too weird," he grumbles. "I remember what my brother and I used to do to our G.I. Joes when we were growing up—so I just can't stand the thought that, all around the world, little kids are putting firecrackers between Worf's legs."

Before heading to the big screen for "Star Trek: Generations," Dorn (who made the move earlier, when he played Worf's grandfather in "Star Trek VI: The Undiscovered Country") says he'll first head to Hawaii to "get massaged within an inch of my life." Then, after the film wraps in June, he plans to meet up for a vacation in Greece with Marina Sirtis and her husband, Michael Lamper, and then join Patrick Stewart for some theatre-hopping in London. If the movie is a hit, there will be future opportunities to do a reunion on-screen, and if it isn't, Dorn and his costars can always get together at *Trek* conventions the world over. "This show is going to be part of our lives for the rest of our lives. It's kind of scary, isn't it? But I promise I am *not* going to be playing Worf when I am 60. And if I do, please shoot me...but only in the leg."

PERSONAL BIO

Birthday: Dec. 9; born in Luling, Texas; raised in Pasadena, California
Family: Single

TELEVISION	FILMS
• *The Mary Tyler Moore Show*	• "Rocky"
• *W.E.B.*	• "Demon Seed"
• *CHiPs*	• "Jagged Edge"
• *Getting By*	• "Star Trek VI: The Undiscovered Country"
• *Hotel*	**PASTIME**
• *Knots Landing*	• Flying with the Blue Angels and F-16 flight manoeuvres
• *Falcon Crest*	
• *Days of Our Lives*	
• *Capitol*	

CHARACTER BIO

LIEUTENANT WORF

2340: Son of Mogh, born on the Klingon homeworld of Qo'noS, older brother of Kurn

2346: Orphaned when his parents are killed in the Khitomer Massacre by the Romulans; rescued by the USS Intrepid; adopted by Sergey Rozhenko and his wife, Helena, and raised on the farm world of Gault

2355: Age of Ascension

2357: First Klingon to enter Starfleet Academy

2365: Assigned to chief of security of the Enterprise

2366: Promoted to full lieutenant; Worf's father, Mogh, is accused of betraying the Klingon Empire at Khitomer; Worf accepts discommendation

2367: Reclaims his father's honor

LEVAR BURTON

When *Star Trek: The Next Generation* hit the air in 1987, *Roots* star LeVar Burton—who was hired to play blind Geordi La Forge—was easily the best-known member of its cast. And maybe that's why he seems the least affected by its cancellation.

"I actually feel great about it," grins Burton. "This has been a very fulfilling seven-year cycle in my life, but I feel in my very being that it's time to move on. Time to do what I've been preparing to do." Which is? "To write, direct and produce my own properties. Sometime around our second season, I realized that if I left this show with nothing but money, I would have blown a tremendous opportunity." So Burton squirreled away his dough and formed his own production company, Eagle Nation Films. His first project out of the hopper: "Cyber 40," a dance technology show that he says is "pretty close to getting sponsorship from Sega—and it might even be distributed by Paramount." But the primary reason he created ENF, Burton says, "was to tell stories that are near and dear to my heart." They include "Dancing in the Sun," a dramatic film about a physician with cancer, and a feature movie based on the book collection "The Life and Teaching of the Masters of the Far East." In addition, the socially conscious Burton will continue hosting duties on PBS's "Reading Rainbow," where, effective with the 11th season, he is also producer. Then, of course, there's "Star Trek: Generations."

"The great thing about the *STNG* experience has been the people. If Paramount wants to pay us every 18 months to get together, make a movie, spend time and laugh, hey, that's fine! But the movies are not going to cause us to stay together. We'd continue to hang out regardless." However, he's the least likely cast member to pop up at a Trekker convention. "There are a few people who do them," Burton says cautiously, "but there aren't that many who really do it with integrity." Besides, he connects with the fans in other ways. "I don't need to go to a convention. I just

TODD GRAY/LGI

have to walk out my door. It's amazing how the popularity of this show has multiplied exponentially every season."

Looking back, Burton's fondest *Trek* memories include "Second Chances" and "The Pegasus" (the episodes he directed), and any opportunity to get out of uniform (especially the holodeck episodes "Elementary, Dear Data," "QPid" and "Hollow Pursuits"). "The Enemy," in which he crawled around in the mud pit trying to find his VISOR, also comes to mind, as do the seventh-season guest appearances by "two people I have an enormous amount of love and respect for": former *Roots* cronies Ben Vereen and Madge Sinclair.

The biggest turning point for Geordi? "Becoming chief engineer," Burton says. "He started out as the navigator, but we needed to find *something* for the poor guy to do. After all, Gene always maintained that the Enterprise was so sophisticated it could fly itself."

CHARACTER BIO

LT.-CMDR. GEORDI LA FORGE

2335: Born on the African Confederation on planet Earth
2357: Graduates from Starfleet Academy, with a major in engineering; serves on the USS Victory
2364: Assigned to the USS Enterprise as a flight controller
2365: Promoted to full lieutenant, assigned the post of chief engineer
2366: Promoted to lieutenant-commander
2368: Believed dead, along with Ensign Ro, when they are accidently rendered invisible by a Romulan cloaking device
2369: Rescues Capt. Montgomery Scott from the transporter beam of the USS Jenolen after 75 years
2370: Fails to rescue his mother, captain of the USS Hera

PERSONAL BIO

Birthday: Feb. 16; born in Landstuhl, Germany
Family: Married to Stephanie Cozart
Academic: USC

TELEVISION
- *Reading Rainbow*
- *Roots*
- "Dummy"
- "One in a Million: The Ron LeFlore Story"
- "Grambling's White Tiger"
- "The Guyana Tragedy: The Story of Jim Jones"
- "Battered"
- "Billy: Portrait of a Street Kid"
- "Roots: The Gift"
- "Liberty"
- "Firestorm: 72 Hours in Oakland"
- "Parallel Lives"

FILMS
- "Looking for Mr. Goodbar"
- "The Hunter"
- "The Supernaturals"

DIRECTOR—*STNG*
- "Second Chances"
- "The Pegasus"

ACHIEVEMENTS
- President of Eagle Nation Films

MAJEL BARRETT

No doubt about it, Majel Barrett is a real pistol—and she's got all cartridges loaded. "I'm very disappointed that I'm not part of the finale—of all people, *I* should have been there," says Barrett, the widow of Gene Roddenberry and the only performer to have spanned all *Star Trek* incarnations. For *STNG*, she created the recurring role of madcap mama Lwaxana Troi, whom she's also played on *DS9*. As a result, Barrett is more than just the "First Lady of *Star Trek*," as the fans have proclaimed her. She is also keeper of the flame.

"Apparently the best way for inadequate talent to achieve recognition is by being negative," huffs Barrett, referring to author Joel Engle's new—and very unauthorized—tell-all biography "Gene Roddenberry: The Man and the Myth Behind Star Trek." In it, Engel paints Roddenberry as a sexually insatiable, widely disliked glory hog who over-hyped his own talents while burying the contributions of those who made them a reality. And he got a few of Roddenberry's former set-side cronies to back this up on the record.

"I was rather shocked to see some of them [quoted in the book], because all during Gene's lifetime they were calling him 'Friend, friend, friend, friend.' And then to hear the venom that comes after he's gone!" Barrett considers Engel (who penned a similarly dark tome about Rod Serling) to be one of those people who'd accuse Santa Claus of

molesting children. "And even if some things in the book are true—or even if everything in the book is true—it should never have [been written]. Gene instilled a hope and a brightness in people. He gave us reason to look forward to the future, and he did it with a great deal of love and energy—so leave it alone! People like [Engel] absolutely disgust me. What he's done reflects more on his own attitude and self-image than that of his subject."

And speaking of hidden agendas, La Barrett has some thoughts on the bizarre cancellation of her husband's last creation, *STNG*. "Paramount has come up with a whole bunch of excuses and reasons—but so far none of them holds water. One [exec] will point in one direction, one will point in the other. I have a feeling it has to do with what goes on behind that little door marked 'Accounting.' Maybe I'm wrong, but I don't think we've heard the truth yet." Though La Barrett has not as yet been asked to take part (even as the computer voice) in either the upcoming film or the third series spinoff *Star Trek: Voyager*, she is hardly sitting home waiting for the phone to ring. In a partnership sure to make loyal Trekkers drool, Barrett has joined forced with Dorothy "D.C." Fontana (a former story editor on the classic series) to create a universe around the character of Ranger—a heroic DNA clone—whom Roddenberry created in the early '70s but never did anything with.

"And we're not huntin' for money," assures Barrett, who has sold the techno-comic book rights to BIG Entertainment (the CD-ROM and animation rights have gone, respectively, to IMB and Disney). The duo has taken Ranger and placed him in a "Magnificent Seven" plot set on a dinosaur-filled planet in the Andromeda galaxy. They've also given him some pretty strange traveling companions—among them an asexual test-tube child and an 18-inch-tall female troublemaker.

And just to make sure she gets her own two cents in, Barrett has signed a deal with Simon and Shuster to pen her own *Trek* memoirs. "Unlike a few other people," says Barrett, "I was here for every minute of it."

STAR TREK BIO

STAR TREK—CLASSIC SERIES
- First Officer—"The Cage," the original pilot
- Nurse Chapel—recurring role (dyed her hair blond)
- Computer Voice—USS Enterprise NCC-1701

STAR TREK—FEATURE MOVIES
- Dr. Chapel—"Star Trek: The Motion Picture"
- Cmdr. Chapel—"Star Trek IV: The Voyage Home"

STAR TREK: THE NEXT GENERATION
- Lwaxana Troi—recurring role (Deanna Troi's mother)
- Computer Voice—USS Enterprise NCC-1701-D

CHARACTER BIO

LWAXANA TROI

2328: Marries Starfleet officer Lieut. Ian Andrew Troi

2329: Birth of daughter Kestra

2336: Gives birth to her second daughter, Deanna; Kestra dies

2364: First visit to the USS Enterprise, for the prearranged marriage of her daughter, Deanna

2365: Pursues Picard, while in the throes of a female Betazoid midlife cycle that quadruples her sex drive

2366: Kidnapped by the Ferengi; Picard must feign jealousy to gain her release

2367: Falls for the scientist Timicin, who must return home to commit ritual suicide

2368: Arrives at her wedding in the nude

2370: Collapses into a coma

WHOOPI GOLDBERG

Among the many people inspired by *Star Trek* was a New York street kid who would grow up and change her name to Whoopi Goldberg. The actress—who plays the enigmatic Guinan on *STNG*—found an early hero in Uhura, the black communications officer played by Nichelle Nichols.

"Not only was Uhura proof that black folks would actually make it into the future—and that was very important for us to believe in back in the '60s—she was beautiful, smart and had power. People listened to her," says Goldberg, whose favorite classic episode was "Plato's Stepchildren," in which Uhura and Kirk (William Shatner) shared TV's first interracial kiss. "Watching Nichelle Nichols made me confident that I could make it, too." So confident that she's gone on to win a Grammy, two Golden Globes, and a Best Supporting Actress Oscar for "Ghost."

Surprisingly, the executives at *STNG* didn't go after Goldberg; it was she who suggested the casting when she got word (via buddy LeVar Burton) that the syndicated revival was going into production—and even then it took more than a year to strike a deal, because nobody thought she was serious. After six seasons, Goldberg describes Guinan as "one part me, one part Yoda and one part Andrei Sakharov." Why does she do it? To be a small part of a television phenomenon. "I'm doing it so my great-great-grandkids can one day watch me on videotape. Hey, if you can't be a Lucy, you may as well be a Guinan!"

Besides, you get to wear really cool hats.

CHARACTER BIO

GUINAN—TEN FORWARD HOST

1800s: Born to an alien race of listeners; possesses an intuitive sense extending beyond linear space and time

1893: Living in San Francisco as a wealthy socialite; entertains Samuel Clemens, meets Data and Picard

2168: Her last encounter with Q prior to 2365

2265: The Borg destroy Guinan's home planet and most of her people

2365: Joins the Enterprise, at Picard's request, to become host of the Ten Forward lounge

2366: Lunges at Q with a fork

2369: With Picard, Ro and Keiko O'Brien, is briefly turned into a 12-year-old

WILL WHEATON

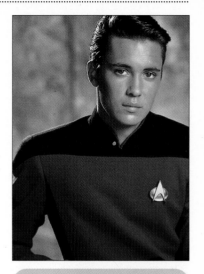

What ever happened to Wil Wheaton? As space teen Wesley Crusher on *STNG*, he was a smash with the younger set—but in the show's fourth season he begged out of his contract to pursue a broader range of roles and, as he puts it, "to go out and experience my life." Unfortunately, the actor—famous for the movie "Stand By Me"—hit some snags along the way.

"The William Morris Agency was sabotaging my career," says Wheaton, now 21. "They were telling casting directors that 'Wil only takes offers now, he doesn't do meetings'—it made me look like the biggest schmuck on the planet." To pay the rent, Wheaton accepted roles in a couple of low-budget big-screen turkeys and then regretted it so much he took a yearlong job at New Tek, a Kansas video firm. While there, the real-life computer whiz helped develop "The Video Toaster"—a system that allows amateurs to turn out TV shows that meet broadcast standards. Says Wheaton proudly, "It does for TV production what the Macintosh did for desktop publishing—makes it accessible and affordable."

He calls his recent return to *STNG* for "Journey's End" an awesome experience—but even though he's "gotten tons of offers" since his Hollywood return, Wheaton has instead enrolled full time in university. "There's so much I want to be able to pass on to my children—and I must start educating myself now," says Wheaton, who's been acting since age 7. "It appalls me that I knew nothing about the Holocaust until I went to see 'Schindler's List.'"

 ## CHARACTER BIO

ENSIGN WESLEY CRUSHER

2349: Born to Jack and Beverly Crusher
2364: Made acting ensign by Picard
2365: Assigned to regular Bridge duty
2366: Admitted to Starfleet Academy, on his second try; but, while helping to secure the release of the kidnapped Deanna and Riker, he misses the Academy transport ship; given a field promotion to full ensign by Picard
2367: Enters Starfleet Academy
2368: First visit back to the Enterprise; Wesley testifies against his squadron after a banned flight manoeuvre causes the death of his friend, Josh Albert
2370: Wesley discovers his true destiny and resigns from Starfleet Academy

DENISE CROSBY

Though her character—security chief Tasha Yar—proved an instantaneous fan favorite during *STNG*'s first season, actress Denise Crosby was so dismayed at her back-burner status in storylines that she personally pleaded with Gene Roddenberry to release her from her contract.

"If he hadn't been alive and holding complete control of the show, there's no way I would have gotten out—Paramount certainly wouldn't have let me go," remembers Crosby. Two months after Roddenberry daringly killed off her character (much to the shock and fury of Trekkers), Crosby won the lead in the eventual box-office hit "Pet Sematary" and her career moved into high gear—but she hadn't seen the last of *STNG*. In Season 3, she was paged to play Tasha in an alternate timeline episode. Then (in a story idea of her own devising) she played Tasha's daughter, Sela, in the two-part cliffhanger that bridged Seasons 4 and 5. "And Sela is still out there somewhere," notes Crosby. "So maybe some day I'll get to play her in a 'Star Trek' movie...or 12."

But first Crosby will once more resurrect Tasha—this time for the series finale. To re-create the character's old look for the past sequences, Crosby decided to chop off her current chin-length hair rather than wear the unconvincing wig Paramount wanted to provide. "I said, 'No, no, no, no—this episode will run in syndication *forever*!' I don't want to tune in when I'm 80 and say, 'Oh, my God, *what* was I thinking? I look like I've got a muskrat on my head!'"

 ## CHARACTER BIO

TASHA YAR (NATASHA)

2337: Born at the Federation colony on Turkana IV

2342: Younger sister, Ishara, is born; Tasha and Ishara are orphaned

2352: Escapes Turkana IV, later joins Starfleet; Ishara stays behind

2364: Assigned to USS Enterprise as chief security officer; is killed by alien Armus on Vagra 2

2366: In an alternative time line, Tasha Yar is discovered alive on the Enterprise NCC-1701-C; when the vessel is sent into the past, Tasha is captured by Romulans, gives birth in 2345 to a daughter, Sela, and is executed in 2349 while attempting to escape

COLM MEANEY

You can't keep a good man down—especially when he's Colm Meaney. On board *The Next Generation* since its inception, the Irish-born actor jumped ship last year when his character, Transporter Chief Miles O'Brien, was made Chief of Operations of *Deep Space Nine*. And even during his *STNG* run, Meaney frequently fled back to Earth to make movies. Among them: "Far and Away," "Under Siege," "The Commitments," and "The Snapper" (which won him a 1993 Golden Globe nomination for Best Actor). In fact, he's spent so much time away from *STNG* that he now considers himself "only a distant relation." But did he take a pass on a finale reunion? No way.

"I was very pleased to be asked—it was a lovely way to round off the whole experience," says Meaney, who will be seen in some of the past sequences of "All Good Things..." And he reports that it was déjà vu. "They hauled everything out of storage. We wore our spacesuits from the first season, and Brent Spiner and I had to sit in these bizarre chairs we'd completely forgotten about." The mood on the set was very joyous. There was a lot of 'Hey, do you remember when...?' We had great laughs remembering the day we first learned how to shake our bodies to make it look like the ship was on the verge of being destroyed."

However, cold reality set in the day after *STNG* wrapped. "I was on the lot doing *DS9*, and I unconsciously walked over to the [*STNG*] set to have a chat with Jonathan Frakes. And his trailer was gone. It was a bit of a shock. They move fast around here."

 ## CHARACTER BIO

MILES O'BRIEN

2364: Assigned to USS Enterprise

2365: Assigned to position of Transporter Chief

2367: Is reunited with Capt. Benjamin Maxwell, his former commanding officer aboard the USS Rutledge; is married to Keiko Ishikawa by Capt. Picard

2368: His daughter, Molly, who is delivered by Worf, is born

2369: Briefly possessed by a disembodied entity from an unsuspected penal colony; is reassigned to Deep Space Nine, where he becomes Chief of Operations

MICHELLE FORBES

After more than a year's absence, Michelle Forbes returned for *The Next Generation*'s next-to-last episode to wrap up her popular role as Ensign Ro. And, to be frank, she was expecting a few mood changes.

"I thought I'd come back towards the end and find the actors at each other's throats—you know, finally see that happy façade broken down. And, unfortunately," says Forbes with a wink, "it was exactly the same as I'd left it—the rats! The myth had *not* been broken." Such rock-solid, long-standing camaraderie, she says, is very rare in television. "I've seen people on other series who just get burnt out and bitter and start hating each other. Sure, there were politics at *STNG*, but the actors all rose above it. After seven years, they're still going out to dinner."

Forbes says the secret, in part, is the fun factor: "Though the show deals with politics and some very serious matters of the heart, the really great appeal is that we're hired to be kids. They actually *paid* me to fly in a spaceship and talk to monsters," says Forbes, who lists Ro's first and final episodes as "the most pleasurable because they were the most profound."

But Forbes, who never mastered technobabble, is a little gun-shy of those Trekker conventions. "They sort of wig me out a bit, because I haven't been on the show enough to know any of the technical information. I can never answer the audience questions. I'm like, 'Uhhh...I don't know...next question?...Uhhh...I don't know...Yes, you in the third row in the pointed ears...Uhhh...I don't know.' It's a nightmare!"

CHARACTER BIO

ENSIGN RO LAREN

2340: Born on Bajor
2347: Witnesses her father's torture and murder by the Cardassians
2368: Assigned to USS Enterprise after earlier court martial for disobeying orders, which led to eight deaths on an Away Team mission; believed dead, along with Geordi, when they are rendered invisible by a Romulan cloaking device
2369: Is accidentally turned into a 12-year-old, along with Picard, Guinan and Keiko O'Brien
2370: As an undercover operative, finds her loyalty split between the Federation and the vigilante Maquis

JOHN de LANCIE

In assessing his role as Q, the recurring bad boy of *The Next Generation*, John de Lancie compares himself to the Marx Bros.—but, mind you, he does it in all modesty. "What did they do? Six films? And they're all considered great classics," says de Lancie. "Well, the fact of the matter is, they only did two that are actually terrific but because they made so few, people love them all. I think I've enjoyed a bit of that with Q. My following is quite disproportionate to the times I've played him."

Though de Lancie's appearance on the series finale marks the eighth time he's taken the role, he says he's "quite happy remaining on the periphery." But he has no qualms about attending those *Trek* conventions. "I use the money to give myself the freedom to do things I know are kind of crazy," says the actor, who (after "All Good Things...") will bypass film and TV jobs for two months to film "Redwoods," an environmental IMAX motion picture to be shot in Northern California's redwood forests. "I could make more money staying here," he admits, "but it's a story that's close to my heart."

In its advance hype for *DS9*, Paramount tantalized Trekkers with the juicy news that de Lancie's Q would be making a crossover appearance. Will the studio do the same with *Voyager*? "Purrrr-haps," de Lancie coos, noting that drop-ins from *STNG* would be rather tricky, since the *Voyager* crew will be lost in space. "Rick [Berman] has said that—at least in terms of logic—the only crossover character could be Q. But then logic doesn't always reign supreme—in science fiction or the entertainment industry."

CHARACTER BIO

Q

2364: Tries Picard and crew for the crimes of mankind; tempts Rikers with the powers of the Q
2365: Sends Enterprise to a distant galaxy, where they encounter the Borg
2366: Takes refuge aboard the Enterprise, when he is briefly kicked out of the Q for his past misdeeds
2367: Sends Picard and crew into Sherwood Forest as Robin Hood and his Merry Men
2369: Returns to the Enterprise to indoctrinate a young Q; meets Picard in the afterlife and returns him to life
2370: For the second time, puts Picard on trial for crimes of mankind

FACTOIDS

WHAT EVER HAPPENED TO?

• **TELEVISION:** So much for the 500-channel universe. Beyond the year 2040, television no longer survived as a form of entertainment. Instead, the holodeck provides endless hours of fantasy enjoyment, and the on-board computer stores recorded music and an extensive selection of video books.

• **BASEBALL:** Although major-league baseball became international by the early 21st century—and Buck Bokai, a shortstop turned third baseman for the London Kings broke Joe DiMaggio's hitting record in 2026—the final World Series was played and won by the London Kings in 2042. Nonetheless, the game continued to have appeal as a hobby—Wesley Crusher and Jake Sisko (*DS9*) both learned the game from their fathers—and as an investment, with collector Kivas Fajo ("The Most Toys") counting Roger Maris's trading card among his most prized possessions.

• **GAMES:** While poker and three-dimensional chess are well known in the 24th century, new games include Strategema ("Peak Peformance"), a game of mental strategy, and Parrises Squares ("11001001"), an athletic game involving competition between two teams of four players.

• **MONEY:** Cold, hard cash is a thing of the past, replaced by Federation credits in 2161, when the Federation was established. Of course, gold-pressed latinum still comes in handy when dealing with the Ferengi.

EMMY AWARDS

YEAR	NOMINATIONS	WINS
1987-88	7	3
1988-89	8	2
1989-90	9	2
1990-91	10	2
1991-92	7	5
1992-93	5	2
Total*	46	16

* Does not include nominations or wins for 1993-94. The Emmys are scheduled for Sept. 12, 1994.

TREK FACTS

AVERAGE COST PER CLASSIC EPISODE
$180,000 US

AVERAGE COST PER *STNG* EPISODE
$1.5 MILLION US

TIME IT TAKES TO APPLY DATA'S MAKEUP
75 MINUTES

NUMBER OF EPISODES DIRECTED BY CAST MEMBERS
16

NUMBER OF *TREK* NOVELS SOLD
30 MILLION

***TREK* RETAIL SALES IN PAST FIVE YEARS**
$750 MILLION US

NUMBER OF *TREK* CONVENTIONS PER YEAR IN NORTH AMERICA
OVER 3000

FEDERATION FUNNIES

"Do you think that Capt. Kirk is getting a little older?...The other day, he went almost 300 million miles with his left blinker on!"—**Jay Leno (March 23, 1994)**

"We all know that the original crew is getting a little older!...I hear many of the laser weapons on board are controlled by the clapper!"—**David Letterman (March 31, 1994)**

"A scheduled interview between Ross Perot and Sam Donaldson was canceled last week. The network was concerned that people may confuse it with a bad episode of Star Trek, where Spock meets a Ferengi!"—**Jay Leno (March 23, 1994)**

" I hear Vice-President Al Gore is going to appear on STNG. I think he's Data's long-lost cousin!"—**Jay Leno (March 23, 1994)**

CROSS-COUNTRY TREK-UP

TOTAL NUMBER OF HOURS OF *STAR TREK* AVAILABLE PER WEEK IN CANADA*

	STAR TREK	STNG	DS9	TOTAL HRS.
HALIFAX	7	6	1	14
SAINT JOHN	6	7	2	15
MONTREAL	6	6	1	13
OTTAWA/HULL	6	7	1	14
TORONTO/HAMILTON	8	12	3	23
LONDON	6	10	3	19
WINNIPEG/BRANDON	7	9	2	18
REGINA/MOOSE JAW	6	1	1	8
CALGARY/LETHBRIDGE	10	8	6	24
EDMONTON	10	8	3	21
VANCOUVER/VICTORIA	7	13	3	23

* Spring 1994

SPACE TREKKERS

Each week, millions of armchair astronauts travel through the galaxies on *Star Trek: The Next Generation*. But in real life, of course, only a handful of people have actually journeyed into space. In the interviews that follow, voyagers from the Challenger, Discovery and Endeavour shuttles—Marc Garneau, Roberta Bondar and Mae Jemison—describe their unique perspective on space travel . . . and *Star Trek*.

by PAUL WELSBY

In 1969, less than two months after Neil Armstrong took the first steps on the moon, the original *Star Trek* series took a giant leap from the airwaves. Ironically, during the year marking the 25th anniversary of Armstrong's Apollo 11 mission, *Star Trek: The Next Generation* is ending a seven-year TV voyage that, for most viewers, was their principal way of seeing outer space.

But what about those viewers who have really been up there? One might expect they'd have little use for Gene Roddenberry's flight of fantasy.

Not so—at least in the case of Marc Garneau, the first Canadian astronaut, who in 1984 blasted off in the space shuttle Challenger as payload specialist. "Going into space today is still pretty primitive compared to what appears on *Star Trek: The Next Generation*. So I watch the show for the same reasons other people watch it," says the Quebec City native. "I haven't been aboard the Enterprise. I've been aboard the space shuttle, which is still a long ways from that."

THE ENTERPRISE...

So exactly what is it about the Enterprise that appeals to Garneau? "I'd certainly like to do some teletransporting," he says of *Star Trek*'s signature "beam me up" device.

"And the main thing, of course, is that they can go at warp speed. That's probably the biggest challenge lying ahead of us in terms of future developments—to be able to get up there at those speeds, so we can indeed go out there and visit different parts of our galaxy and different parts of our universe.

"Because if you look at the shuttle speed, which is Mach 25—impressive by Earth-based standards—it's just creeping insofar as getting even to the closest star.

"When you tell people that it only takes 90 minutes to go around the Earth in the shuttle at Mach 25, they're very impressed. I mean, the idea of going eight kilometres in one second is pretty impressive. But it's nothing like the Enterprise."

FLIGHT OF FANTASY...

And the Enterprise is nothing like reality, a point stressed by fellow Canadian astronaut Dr. Roberta Bondar, who admits to being a little bothered when she talks to kids about space flight, "and they all come in with their *Star Trek* communication buttons on." To be sure, Bondar, a native of Sault Ste. Marie, Ont., who in 1992 roared into space aboard the shuttle Discovery, is more guarded in her praise of *STNG*.

"This is not to be a negative comment," she says. "But with the *Star Trek* series, sometimes I think young people who are so engrossed with videogames and with a lot of blue-screen techniques and the kind of fancy gadgetry that we can do on Earth expect that is the state of affairs. And I think it is very tough for young people to separate reality from science fiction. *Star Trek* is done very, very well, and done very realistically in terms of what we can do ourselves when we see things flying in and out of the screen— and people just assume that is our technology. I don't think people understand where the space program is today. So in one sense it still gives you a flight of fantasy, but when you are really a true space voyager it is not realistic in the sense of what we are able to do right now."

Herself the proud owner of a *Star Trek* communicator badge she received as a Christmas gift ("I treasure

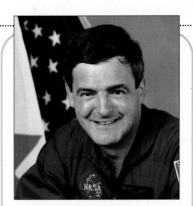

MARC GARNEAU

"I haven't been aboard the Enterprise. I've been aboard the space shuttle, which is still a long ways from that."

it—it's great fun"), Bondar praises *STNG* more for its philosophical and social messages than its high-tech flair. In particular, the efforts of Picard and crew to solve problems with a minimum of violence and a maximum of team effort spring to mind. "When we watch something like *Star Trek*, we can see preserved in there some really good human values to which we would like to attach ourselves," she says. "To me, this and the ability to work with each other are the most positive things [about *STNG*]. Those are the very human things that are the most positive and

ROBERTA BONDAR

"When we watch something like Star Trek, *we can see preserved in there some really good human values to which we would like to attach ourselves."*

are probably better displayed in this particular type of science fiction program than many others."

TRANSPORTER...

The only person to have viewed space from both a real spacecraft *and* a role on the *Star Trek* series is Dr. Mae Jemison. Growing up in Chicago, Jemison watched the original *Star Trek* and longed for the day she would go into space herself. "I knew I was going into space prior to ever seeing *Star Trek*," she says. "I had been watching

the space program for years and had been very interested in it when *Star Trek* debuted. Of course, having a character like Lieut. Uhura [Nichelle Nichols] was very important and was a reaffirming kind of thing. I was one of those people who stubbornly thought it was nonsense that they were only sending men into space. I was only 6 years old, thinking this is ridiculous."

Indeed it was, as Jemison proved on Sept. 12, 1992, when she trekked to the stars aboard the shuttle Endeavour. Eight months later, she appeared as a transport officer on the *STNG* episode titled "Second Chances." For Jemison, her "return" to space was pure fun ("My line was something like 'Phase distortion is decreasing. Transport window will be open in 26 seconds, sir'."). As for which piece of *STNG* technology she'd like to play with in real life, she says, "I think everyone's favorite gadget, if you can call it that, is the whole Enterprise, just because of where it allows you to go. And of that I guess the transporter. How many of us would love to go somewhere without luggage, just show up where you are and not end up having to take a bus?"

Unlike Bondar, Jemison has no problem with the fantasy world of *STNG*. "I think fantasy is beneficial, whether it's looking at fantasy in science or reading fantasy in novels," she explains. "There are novels that have had great impact on the world that were someone's fantasy, but yet they reflect quite a bit about humans and our makeup and what we hope and wish for—and sometimes the best and the worst of us...It allows us to hope for better things. I think what was so wonderful about the *Star Trek* series, both when I was a little girl and watching the original *Star*

Trek—and now *Star Trek: The Next Generation* and *Deep Space Nine*—is here's a universe where people hope to do better, and we have a future where we manage to get beyond some very large stumbling blocks."

WARP SPEED...

For Garneau, one such obstacle to overcome is the speed of light, which he considers the equivalent of Warp 1 (see the chart below). Does he think we will we ever achieve Warp 1?

"Yes, we absolutely will," he says. "Or just underneath it. There are people who say it's impossible to go the speed of light—you have to know your relativity theory to get into that kind of argument—but that you can approach it. But yes, I believe we will. It would be nice to think we could go several warps, because that's really going to be what we need to do to get out there and look around."

Make it so.

MAE JEMISON
—on the transporter

"How many of us would love to go somewhere without luggage, just show up where you are and not end up having to take a bus?"

SPEED	NO. X SPEED OF LIGHT	Kм-H (millions)	EARTH TO MOON (seconds)
WARP 1	1	1078	1.34
WARP 2	10	11,000	0.13
WARP 3	39	42,000	0.03
WARP 4	102	109,000	0.013237
WARP 5	214	230,000	0.006291
WARP 6	392	423,000	0.003426
WARP 7	656	707,000	0.002049
WARP 8	1024	1,103,000	0.001313
WARP 9	1516	1,630,000	0.000886

Speeds and times according to "THE STAR TREK ENCYCLOPEDIA" by Michael Okuda, Denise Okuda and Debbie Mirek

READER TRIBUTES

When it comes to loyal Trekkers, TV GUIDE readers number in the thousands—all eager to share their farewell tributes to the cast, crew and creators of *STNG*. On the following pages, we present the best of our readers' poems, drawings, photos and cartoons. We've also included reader responses to two topics—"How *Star Trek* Changed My Life" and "I Married a Trekker"—raised in our March 5 issue. The letters are humorous, serious, touching and sweet—and we think you'll enjoy each and every one. Our thanks to everyone who took part.

HOW *STAR TREK* CHANGED MY LIFE

Kimberly Heaton,
Newmarket, Ont.

"B.C. (before children), my husband and I were avid viewers of STNG. Now, it seems that our 2¹/₂-year-old son has become a Trekkie, too! Each night after dinner Billy asks for 'Capin

Acard.' That's changed the way I communicate with my son. Now, if I really want him to do something, I need only tell him that Capt. Picard does it. Suddenly, 'Capin Acard' puts on his own socks and shoes, takes a nap, and tidies up his toys. It may sound rather trivial, but Capt. Picard

Rob Grant, Hamilton, Ont.

Geordi La Forge, Chief Engineer,
Enjoys exploring the final frontier.
Oh yes, this Scotty of the Next Generation
Repairs everything with determination.
Don't hide anything from this Enterpriser.
It just won't work;
*   he'll see it with his VISOR.*

Tracey Telgen,
Arnprior, Ont.
(pencil sketch)

Gord Roberts,
Ancaster, Ont.
(color pencil)

has sure worked a few minor miracles in our household! My only wish now is that the reruns will remain in syndication long enough for First Officer Murray to follow the same directives as his brother."

Patricia King, Lively, Ont.

"My daughter, Erin, inspired by the genius of the STNG series, began writing her own science fiction novel in January 1993. Only 12 years old at the time, she has relentlessly pursued this task for the past 15 months, and at page 367 (longhand) is nearing completion of a truly mesmerising

tale. At 13, she has 'bodly gone' where few teens have gone before— into the world of imagination and, eventually, into a career that will allow her to 'write well and prosper'! Thank you, Gene! Good luck, Erin! P.S.: Would Paramount be interested in the movie rights?"

Catherine MacLeod,
Tatamagouche, N.S.

"In 1973, at the age of 12, I decided to write an original Trek story. That decision changed my life. My first story was terrible, but it was the first thing I'd ever written that wasn't

Allison Durno, Jodi Krangle, Debbie Ridpath Ohi (Urban Tapestry), Orangeville, Ont.

A Neurotic Love Song
Robert Redford has the chin,
Mel Gibson has the eyes,
Sean Connery has the experience,
and Arnie has the size.
But they all can't compare
to one very Special Guy
who may have zero hair but
makes my hormones fry...

Chorus:
Jean-Luc, Jean-Luc
You're my kind of mah-an
You say (spoken): Earl Grey...HOT
Like no one else can.

Forget about Lwaxana
and that hussy Beverly.
Eline and Vash are goners,
Your heart belongs to me.

When they say you're fictional,
it cuts me like a knife
They tell me I'm a loony,
that I should get a life.
But they can't understand the
passion that we share.
I want to lie beside you,
run my fingers though your...

assigned by an English teacher. I wrote something because I wanted to. What a RUSH! Twelve may be young to know what you want to do with your life, but since Star Trek started me writing, there's never been any doubt."

Jeff Jacques, Nepean,Ont.

"During the third season of STNG, I became a big fan of that show. Now, as STNG comes to the end of its seventh and final season on TV, I find myself buying toys again. Of course, at age 24, I don't consider them toys—they're collectibles. I must admit, I feel slightly awkward walking up to the cashier with items like action figures, phasers and tricorders. But sacrifices must be made! My everyday life has also been affected to some extent. I try to maintain that perfect Rikeresque posture; I lapse into a Picardian accent when I recite captain's logs, and I occasionally sprinkle the word 'indeed' into my everyday verbalizations; I find myself performing the 'Picard manoeuvre' with my shirts and jackets, even when it isn't necessary. I even tried drinking Earl Grey tea once, but I didn't continue with that. Live long and prosper, Star Trek, and I look forward to the 50th anniversary in 2017."

Dana Dionne, Langley, B. C.

"The next mission for the Starship Enterprise and its crew members is going on in our home. The mission: the invasion and takeover of our doll room. Can you just picture the situation? These beautiful, innocent baby dolls, surrounded by Romulans, Klingons and other such creatures? A real pretty picture...NOT!"

Lorraine Boisvert, Ormocto, N. B.

"My husband is in the military and was sent to Bosnia for a tour of duty. Before he left, he asked that I record STNG so that when he returned home he could watch the episodes. For the next six months, I made sure that once a week the VCR would run. I'll never forget the look of happiness and contentment on my husband's face as he sat on the couch with our 8-month-old son and watched the series."

Mrs. Janet Stevens, Comox, B. C.

"In the sping of '92, I was diagnosed with breast cancer. After surgery, I had to have radiation treatment. The treatment centre is 150 miles from where I live, so I would be away from my family from Monday to Friday every week for a period of five weeks. My first weekend home, I watched STNG with my grandson. For an hour, I was 'transported' away from my fears and my problems. I became involved with the excitement that took place on the Enterprise. We watched STNG four times that weekend, and the relief and peace of mind that it gave me was something that I feel very special about. To this day, I do not miss an episode, and I still feel wonderfully transported. I'm a Trekker forever."

Bernard Reischl,
Montreal, Que.
(ink drawing)

Sara Whelan,
age 7,
Arnprior, Ont.
(paper collage)

Bernard Reischl,
Montreal, Que.
(ink drawing)

The Strong Family Trekkers: Cheryl and Russ Strong and their two children, Winnipeg, Man.

I MARRIED A TREKKER

Daniel Lyon, Toronto, Ont.

"As the husband of a Trekker, I have observed that Trekkers are a lot like Tribbles. They may look sweet and harmless, but before you know it they've taken over your life and eaten all your food. It is a mystery to me that Trekkers not only tolerate, but actually enjoy, watching the same episodes dozens of times. The only reason that no one has applied to the CRTC for a MuchTrek channel is that Trekkers prefer to control every channel rather than just one."

Melanie Langrehr,
Kitchener, Ont.

"My boyfriend, David, and I have been going out now for almost a year. When we first started seeing each

other, I carried a strong dislike for Star Trek. *David is a large fan. We spent—and continue to spend—two hours every weeknight and an hour every Saturday and Sunday staying at home. Just try making plans between 6 P.M. and 8 P.M. But I have to say I've begun to grow somewhat fond of the show. My first convention is coming up, and I've received my uniform top to wear. I'm 'First Officer'—the rank under 'Capt. David Rush'.*"

Susan Lee, Strathroy, Ont.

"*My fiancé is Kevin. He is truly a* Star Trek *fan. We must watch STNG every day, even repeats. Our Christmas tree had* Star Trek *ornaments on it. If it were up to Kevin, that's all that would be on it. Our living room has a large Enterprise model on the china cabinet with* Star Trek *figurines surrounding it. Our family room has a large poster which says, 'All I Need to Know About Life I Learned From* Star Trek.' *We're getting married in June, and, yes, the theme of the wedding is—you guessed it—Star Trek.*"

Cynthia A. Mationsky,
Brandon, Man.

"*It wasn't until STNG made its television debut that I really began to take an interest in* Star Trek. *Shortly after that, I met an avid Trekker by the name of Mark, and we fell in love. Only then did I become a true fan. That was six years ago, and we are just now beginning to plan our wedding. With a little encouragement from Mark, we've decided to*

Alisa Villemure,
Campbell River, B.C.

An Ode to Star Trek: The Next Generation
Dear Mr. Roddenberry, thank you,
Where ever you now may be,
For the gift of the world of adventure
and for all the fun it's given me.

Starfleet's a wonderful world
With no excessive violence or crime,
No talk of racial problems
Something we need in our time.

A group of people who are courageous,
Loyal, trustworthy and strong,
They travel the universe over
To help others feel they belong.

We're tired of soaps and talk shows,
Of inane sitcoms galore,
Of real-life stories of heartbreak
We needed this fantasy lore.

Heather Jarvis,
Port Coquitlam, B.C.

Farewell to Star Trek
(The Legend Will Live On)
For seven years we've followed you
Throughout the thick and thin
And remember everything you've done
And how close to death you've been.

But as all good things, I suppose
This too must come to an end
And although it may be very painful
We must say goodbye again.

Valerie Herd,
Niagara Falls, Ont.
(ink drawings)

Shannon Desjardins, Delta, B. C.

Star Trek Adventures
It was just before Star Trek
and all through the house
No one was working,
not even a mouse.
The TV was turned on to
Star Trek *with care,*
In hopes that Jean-Luc Picard
would be there.
The children were sitting
all quiet on the floor.
Then Mother and Father
came in through the door.

The commercials were over,
and on came the song.
We all said the words and
we all sang along.
When out on the porch
there arose such a clatter
We sprang from our show to
see what was the matter.
Away to the door
we all flew in a flash
And opened the door at
the end of our dash.

When what to our wondering
eyes should appear?
The Enterprise Crew!
Goodness, they were HERE!
Deanna was there and she cried,
"Oh, the pain!"

Riker stepped up
and he held her in vain.
When the Captain of captains
consoled, "It's all right,"
She said, "No it isn't; my
uniform's too tight!"

Well, I and my family
knew not what to say
And it seemed like we would
just stand there all day
Until Geordi La Forge,
the hero of the week,
Saw a kitchen appliance and
cried, "Let me peek!"
But Worf, who was eager
to continue the trip
Growled, "Just grab her and
get back to the ship!"

Captain Picard announced,
to my total surprise
That I belonged on his ship,
on the Enterprise!
For as I was the captain of a
Startrekking group
And an active member
of a large Starfleet troupe
The Enterprise had traveled
way back through time
Which brings me to the end
of this Startrekking rhyme.

have a Star Trek *wedding. I've run into a bit of a snag, though. Mark would love to have Klingon dishes served for the meal, but I don't know where to begin. Would Worf have any recipe hints he could pass along?"*

Meg Mumford, Victoria, B.C.

"I live with a Trekker. I am his mother. He is almost 5 years old. Christopher began to absorb Star Trek *in the womb. After birth, he watched new episodes and reruns with me. Now I, his father and his younger sister watch with him. Capt. Picard's picture and a poster of the Bridge crew adorn the kitchen, and drawings and cutouts of the Enterprise decorate Chris's bedroom. We trip over his* Star Trek *models in every corner of the house. Some days, I feel as if I live on the Enterprise. Or rather, I feel as though I inhabit two worlds—Chris will ask a question about STNG characters or stories as often as he inquires about real situations. From the time he began to talk, I found myself saying things like, 'On* Star Trek, *it's like such and such. In this world, it's like such and such.' We finally bought one of the books describing the episodes, and I boned up. Now I use the stories as a reference point for discussing events in 'our' world. Chris can appreciate the concepts of bravery, love, jealousy, war, whatever, if we make a quick reference: 'Remember the story where Q visits the Enterprise?' In case you may be wondering, Chris is also keenly interested in books and learning to read. So I was not too worried when, on a recent park excursion, he remarked enthusiastically, 'This is just like the holodeck!' Reference, Part 2 of 'Encounter at Farpoint,' Mom!"*

Jennifer Ellis, Brantford, Ont.

Ode to Data
Data never complains
About being put in danger
Because he can't feel the fear
Upon meeting a stranger.

You must long for a simpler time
When you could laugh or sob
Sitting in a Night Court room
Answering to Bob.

I wonder if you realized
The adulation you would conceive
For playing a character
incapable of giving
The love that he receives.

What is it about you
That makes us fall at your feet?
The mystery you project,
The secrets that you keep?

For others I cannot speculate,
But for me the reason is stark.
Besides charm and talent,
I like men who glow in the dark.

James Corbett, Calgary, Alta.

My Salute to Star Trek: The Next Generation
Now for Data
Our favourite of all,
He was certainly the best-selling
STNG doll.
He was as strong as 10 men
and his intellect couldn't be beat,
So why was he still a lieutenant
After 26 years in the 'Fleet?

GAMES

TEST YOUR KLINGON

You can always tell a Trekker by the Klingon he or she speaks. Especially since linguist Marc Okrand perfected the language and created "The Klingon Dictionary" (see page 52). And now we bring you the first Klingon word puzzle, composed of 80 Klingon words or phrases (with English translation). Words are formed in a straight line—forward, backward, up, down or diagonally—without skipping over letters. Letters may be used more than once and sometimes overlap. Those letters not used to solve the puzzle can be used to form an additional eight mystery Klingon phrases. Good luck. (For the solution to the puzzle and the mystery phrases, see page 128.)

batlh	honor (noun)	**jIH**	viewing screen (n)
blmoHqu'	"You're very ugly"	**jol**	transport beam (n)
boq	alliance (n)	**leng**	trip, voyage (n)
chetvI'	torpedo tube (n)	**leSpoH**	shore leave (n)
chuyDaH	thrusters (n)	**loDnI'**	brother (n)
Daq	eavesdrop (verb)	**logh**	space (n)
Daw'	revolt, revolution (n)	**lotlhwI'**	rebel (n)
De'	data, information (n)	**lurDech**	tradition (n)
Degh	helm (n)	**maghwI'**	traitor (n)
De'wI'	computer (n)	**may'Duj**	battle cruiser (n)
DIb	privilege (n)	**mIqta'**	machinery (n)
DIvI'	Federation (n)	**mup**	impact, strike (v)
Dol	entity (n)	**mu'**	word (n)
Dum	nap (v)	**ngoq**	code (n)
Dung	area overhead (n)	**noch**	sensor (n)
ghol	adversary, opponent (n)	**no'**	ancestors (n)
ghom	encounter, meet (v)	**peD**	snow (v)
HeDon	parallel course (n)	**pu'HIch**	phaser pistol (n)
HeS	commit a crime (v)	**pujwI'**	weakling (n)
HeSwI'	criminal (n)	**Qapla'**	success (n)
HIjol	"Beam me aboard"	**Qargh**	fissure (n)
HIp	uniform (n)	**qawHaq**	memory banks (n)
Hong	impulse power (n)	**QeDpIn**	science officer (n)
Hoqra'	tricorder (n)	**QeyHa'moH**	loosen (v)
HoSchem	energy field (n)	**qIbHes**	galactic rim (n)
jegh	give up, surrender (v)	**QI'**	military (n)

y	I	w	b	I	l	o	g	h	j	p	Q	e	y	H	a'	m	o	H	j
l	u	r	D	e	c	h	e	n	g	q	I	u'	h	e	b	e'	c	o	u
t	h	Q	u	h	g	e	j	g	o	a	q	H	h	S	v	n	u	S	D
a	l	j	j	n	l	e	S	p	o	H	a	D	y	u	h	c	b	c	y'
I'	I	h	e	I	H	q	e	g	o	w	I	l	o	h	g	h	n	h	a
h	w	l	I	b	j	o	I	m	r	a	t	j	I	H	a	e	g	e	m
S	g	h	b	n	I	D	l	b	o	q	r	n	o	c	h	t	o	m	j
h	a	n	l	b	g	b	I	l	H	h	u'	n	D	I	I'	v	q	u	p
q	l	r	a	t	e	a	H	v	c	e	g	a	S	o'	w	I'	w	a'	r
j	a	t	Q	m	o	a	n	I	I'	Q	s	q	q	u'	w	n	a	b	y'
u	D	D	a	a'	r	l	H	e	D	o	n	l	a	e'	u	j	j	o	t
D	u	I	p	b	v	u'	o	a	o	q	h	u	D	S	o	n	o	Q	I'
Q	t	t	u	a	p	H	q	p	y	g	I'	v	I	t	l	I'	l	h	w
e	u	v	D	u	n	g	r	D	u	v	a	e	H	y	w	u	Q	I	m
v	u	q	m	o	h	g	a'	r	I	D	I	n	l	S	b	n	u	u	u
e	q	o	n	t	e	l	o	D	H	b	a	g	e	n	I	p	D	e	Q
S	e'	b	o	t	l	o	o'	b	j	a	D	H	o	v	D	h	e	a	a
D	D	D	e	g	h	D	n	a	q	a	a	o	I'	w	j	u	p	w	r
u	u	g	h	o	m	n	a'	r	e	t	w'	m	l	u'	t	l	u	a	g
j	u	D	Q	o	t	I'	w	h	g	a	m	I	q	t	a'	H	m	u'	h

qIQ	mutiny (v)	toQDuj	Bird of Prey (vessel) (n)
Qob	danger (n)	'urmang	treason (n)
QonoS	log, journal (n)	vengHom	village (n)
QuD	insurrection (n)	veSDuj	warship (n)
QumwI'	communications device (n)	veQDuj	garbage scow (n)
qup	elder (n)	voHDajbo'	ransom (n)
ra'ghomquv	High Command (n)	vub	hostage (n)
ra'wI'	commander (n)	vulqan	Vulcan (planet) (n)
rugh	antimatter (n)	vutpa'	galley (n)
Saqghom	landing party (n)	wIy	tactical display (n)
So'wI'	cloaking device (n)	wuQ	headache, have a headache (v)
Sun	discipline	yaH	duty station (n)
tera'	Earth (n)	yuQjIjDIvI'	United Federation of Planets (n)
tlhIngan	Klingon (n)		
toDuj	courage, bravery (n)		

TEST YOUR *NEXT GENERATION* TRIVIA

by Naomi Boulton

(For answers, see page 124)

1 What is Picard's command to the computer when he wants a drink?

2 Where was the Enterprise built?

3 In which episode did a slow-motion time bubble inadvertently save the Enterprise from being blown to bits by the Romulans?

4 Which actress played a bride in Korea and on the Enterprise?

5 Who is Data's most famous human nemesis, and how was he created?

6 How did Worf's family lose its honor?

7 How did the Enterprise stop the Borg from attacking Earth?

8 Which former *Dallas* star played Tasha Yar's sister?

9 How many members of his family has Data met?

10 Which former *Days of Our Lives* soap star always gets Capt. Picard's lather up?

11 Who is Alexander, and how did his mother die?

12 This enterprising crew member also loves to entertain children. Who is he, and what's his other show?

13 How are Beverly's and Jean-Luc's pasts connected?

14 What is Data's storage capacity?

15 She hangs out on Risa, makes deals with Ferengi, and in her free time picks up Federation staff. Who is she?

16 Who took 90 years to bring his ship out of a time loop?

17 She was raped by a Romulan, but her daughter later joined the Romulans to invade Vulcan.

18 What do Odan and Riker have in common?

19 Which Canadian actor kidnapped Data as the perfect addition to his collection?

20 What killed Jeremy's mother, and who adopted him?

21 Who wouldn't save his own life for the love of Lwaxana Troi?

22 Name Geordi's fantasy date and the woman who plays her.

23 When does Wesley finally leave for Starfleet Academy, and why do we meet up with him again?

24 What is Ensign Ro's home world, and who are its enemies?

25 Describe the goriest scene in *Star Trek* history and name the episode.

26 Which media personality played a Klingon tormentor in Worf's coming-of-age ceremony?

27 He rides the Enterprise and protects the crew, but he used to ride a motorcycle and protect his city. Name him and his former show.

28 What is Lieut. Barclay's nickname, and what is his favorite pastime?

29 When did Data officially become an independent being and cease to be the property of Starfleet?

30 This actress played a sometimes frigid psychiatrist, but as an alien she couldn't get enough, especially from Riker. Who is she?

31 Which race did Kevin destroy?

32 Who are those peekaboo-breasted Klingon sisters, and why do they want to destroy peace in the Empire?

33 Which former *Falcon Crest* hunk now mans the Enterprise?

34 Who makes Picard cringe at the mere mention of her name?

35 What does VISOR stand for?

36 Which testy commander took over the Enterprise from Picard and sent him on a kamikaze mission?

37 Who was Wesley's extremely versatile first love?

38 Why did Worf want Alexander to kill him?

39 Which famous Martian is now at Starfleet Academy?

40 He plays a TV attorney, but in the future he has more power than the Supreme Court. Who is he?

41 What was the name of the planet where Picard discovered his inner light?

42 Who is Data's beloved?

43 Which lieutenant's dog turns into a big, hungry blob?

44 Why did Lwaxana arrive at her wedding naked, and what happened to the groom?

45 She's Jean-Luc's long-lost love.

46 When did a little girl's imaginary friend become real?

47 Who was stored in a cocoon to protect her from mating with unsuitable men?

48 He may have written "A Brief History of Time," but what he really wanted was to play poker with Data. Who is he?

49 Name Worf's foster parents.

50 How many decks does the Enterprise have?

COLLECTOR'S CORNER

Earning millions each year for Paramount, the *Star Trek* franchise is not just movies and syndicated reruns. With over 500 different products licensed in Canada alone, there's no shortage of manufacturers willing to trade on the *Star Trek* name. The following pages contain just a sample of what's available at retail, by mail order and, of course, at conventions. A number of these products are also available through the Official Star Trek Fan Club of Canada magazine, at a discount to club members. For a complete list of more than 500 *Star Trek* licensed products, send $3 to: The Official Star Trek Fan Club of Canada, c/o PPFD Merchandising, 89 Mills Rd., Ajax, Ont. L1S 7L3 (1-800-263-4678).

BOOKS

The Klingon Dictionary—The Official Guide to Klingon Words and Phrases (Pocket Books, $13)—by Marc Okrand. Having created the Klingon language for the *Star Trek* feature films, linguist Okrand provides a complete sourcebook of Klingon syntax, phrases and pronunciation. Clever without being daunting, Okrand's Klingon phrases will guarantee the user's getting the last word in any argument. Audio cassettes also available; see audio section, page 54.

Star Trek Chronology—The History of the Future (Pocket Books, $18) —by Michael Okuda and Denise Okuda. A highly entertaining year-by-year history of the *Star Trek* universe by *STNG* scenic art supervisor Okuda and his wife, Denise. With over 500 photos, the book details the significant events, dates and people from *Star Trek*'s past and present, up to *STNG*'s fifth season.

The Star Trek: The Next Generation Companion (Pocket Books, $17) —by Larry Nemecek. A show-by-show

guide to *STNG*—from its inception to the end of its fifth season—providing insightful plot analysis as well as invaluable behind-the-scenes production details. An updated edition by early '95.

Star Trek: The Next Generation Technical Manual (Pocket Books, $18)—by Rick Sternbach and Michael Okuda. An insider's guide to everything you ever wanted to know about the design and specifications of the USS Enterprise NCC-1701-D, provided by the technical consultants to the

The Star Trek Encyclopedia—A Reference Guide to the Future (Pocket Books, hardcover $32; paperback $23)—by Michael Okuda, Denise Okuda and Debbie Mirek. Hot off the press, a must book for any serious Trekker. With over 400 pages and more than 750 photos, charts and diagrams, contains entries on every character, ship, planet, star and alien race from every episode of the classic Star Trek, STNG, DS9 and the first six ST motion pictures. Includes scientific, technological and cultural definitions.

STNG writing staff. Excellent diagrams will prove highly entertaining to budding Starfleet engineers.

Star Trek: The Next Generation—The Final Episode—All Good Things... (Pocket Books, $26)—by Michael Jan Friedman. Novelization of the two-hour series finale. The hardcover collector's edition includes an eight-page color photo insert. On sale the week of May 22, 1994. Also on audio cassette; see audio section, below.

Star Trek: The Next Generation—Debtor's Planet (Pocket Books, paperback $6.99)—by W.R. Thompson. The 30th novel in a series, these are original stories rather than novelizations of STNG episodes, with a new one released every second month. Coming in July, **Foreign Foes**, by David Galanter and Greg Brodeur.

Star Trek: The Next Generation—

Starfleet Academy No. 4—Capture the Flag (Minstrel Books, $4.99)—by John Vornholt. For younger Trekkers (Grades 3 to 6), the fourth in a series of novels set at Starfleet Academy, San Francisco, featuring the adventures of cadets Worf and Geordi La Forge. Coming in July, **Atlantis Station**, by V.E. Mitchell.

The Best of Star Trek: The Next Generation (DC Comics, $26.95)—by Michael Jan Friedman and John de Lancie. STNG's comic book adventures.

AUDIO

Star Trek: The Next Generation—The Final Episode—All Good Things... (Simon & Schuster Audio, $22)—by Michael Jan Friedman. Read by Jonathan Frakes (Riker) and featuring sound effects and an original score. On

POCKET BOOKS (2)

Conversational Klingon (Simon & Schuster Audio, $13)—by Marc Okrand. An audio companion to Okrand's **Klingon Dictionary**, featuring the author and actor Michael Dorn (Worf). For beginners, the cassette provides instruction on proper voice inflection and pronunciation, sentence structure and grammar as well as key Klingon words for emergencies.

Power Klingon—Mastering the Language of Warriors (Simon & Schuster Audio, $13)—by Barry Levine and Marc Okrand. Also featuring the author and actor Michael Dorn. For more advanced speakers, this cassette includes an original phrase booklet and promises to teach the user to think like a warrior—in Klingon, of course.

sale the week of May 22, 1994.

Star Trek: The Next Generation, Vol. 1—Encounter at Farpoint (GNP Crescendo Records, CD $18.99, cassette $14.98)—Original TV soundtrack of the pilot episode. Also available: **Vol. 2—Best of Both Worlds I and II**; **Vol. 3—Yesterday's Enterprise**, **Unification** (Emmy winner for Best Original Score); and **Hollow Pursuits**. All three volumes also avail-

able as a collector's box set.

Ol' Yellow Eyes Is Back (Select, CD $21.99)—Brent Spiner—A collection of standards, including "Zing! Went the Strings of My Heart," sung by Spiner (Data), a baritone and former Broadway musical performer ("Sunday in the Park With George"). Backup vocals by the Sunspots (*STNG* costars LeVar Burton, Michael Dorn, Jonathan Frakes and Patrick Stewart).

GAMES & SOFTWARE

Star Trek: The Next Generation (Sega Genesis, $70; Nintendo Super NES, $99)—Both games feature neat Enterprise-type graphics and Away Teams made up of *STNG* crew members. On a more sophisticated scale, IBM users with CD-ROM can look forward to Spectrum Holobyte's *STNG* game ($110), available in June.

Star Trek: The Next Generation Interactive VCR Video Board Game —A Klingon Challenge (Canada Games, $39.99)—For three to six players, ages 8 and up. An on-screen Klingon warrior hijacks the USS Enterprise, and, as part of the crew, players race to regain control of the ship. A different game each time.

Star Trek: How to Host a Mystery (Canada Games, $24.99)—A board game that invites you aboard the Enterprise to solve a mystery.

Star Trek: The Next Generation Font Pack (Bitstream, $26)—The Mac-based program features the series' well-known typefaces, emblems and alien symbols. Also available for PCs using Windows 3.1.

MERCHANDISE

Star Trek: The Next Generation Micro Machines (TeeGee Toys, $8.99 to $42.99)—For ages 4 and up, 15 miniature models of *STNG* starships including Ferengi, Klingon, Romulan, Cardassian and Borg. Five sets of three models each, and a collector's set featuring all 15 models, with a bonus USS Enterprise NCC-1701-A.

Star Trek: The Next Generation Model Kits (Ertl Canada, from $12 to $20)—Several models available, including the world's best-selling USS Enterprise, a Klingon Battle Cruiser and special *Star Trek* 25th-anniversary sets.

Star Trek: The Next Generation Character Model Kits (Polydata Resources, $45 to $50)—Six characters available, including Picard, Data and Worf, each model stands 12 inches tall. Coming this summer: Locutus of Borg and Gowron.

Star Trek: The Next Generation Bookplates (Antioch, $5.95, box of 30)—One of a series, the bookplate

VIDEO/LASER DISC

Star Trek: The Next Generation —Encounter at Farpoint (Vol. 1) (Paramount Home Video, VHS, $19.95)—*STNG*'s pilot episode. Available for single purchase up to Vol. 38 (**The Royale**). On a continuity-program basis, featuring two episodes per tape, Columbia House Video has Vols. 1 to 60 (**The Perfect Mate; Imaginary Friend**), with volumes shipped every six to eight weeks. No word yet on when Columbia will have the remaining 58 episodes. Pioneer Laser Disc ($59.95), also featuring two episodes per disc, has the first 32 titles.

The Planets (BMG Video, VHS, $19.98)—Narrated by Patrick Stewart, featuring images from Earth's galaxy captured by the unmanned NASA spaceships Pioneer, Mariner, Viking, Voyager, Galileo and Magellan. The cosmic wonders include lunar sunrises, moonscapes, lava lakes and solar flares as the ships fly over Mars and through Saturn's gossamer rings.

Star Trek: The Next Generation Molecular Beam Transporter (Playmates Toys, $49.99)—For ages 4 and up. A sound chip, lights and mirrors simulate the energizing and dematerializing activity of *STNG*'s transporter beam, making figures appear and disappear instantaneously. Includes batteries and technical blueprint.

Also available from Playmates Toys: **Starship Enterprise** ($34.99); **Starship Enterprise Glider** ($16.99); **Starship Excelsior** ($34.99); **Shuttle Goddard** ($39.99); **Klingon Attack Cruiser** ($34.99); **Romulan Warbird** ($34.99); **Ferengi Maurauder** ($34.99); **Borg Ship** ($34.99); **Tricorder** ($15.99); **Phaser** ($15.99); **Phaser Rifle** ($39.99) with Borg training target; **Communicator Walkie Talkie** ($34.99, batteries not included); **Personal Communicator** ($10.99); **Bridge Playset** ($64.99); **Engineering Playset** ($38.99); and more than 40 **Action Figures** ($5.99 each), including the entire crew, significant guest stars, villains and aliens.

features a color photo of the cast and the designation "Property of Starfleet Officer." Also available: *STNG* bookmarks, journal, address book, notebook and memo wipe-off board.

Star Trek: The Next Generation Insignia Collection (Franklin Mint, $660 U.S.)—The complete set of 12 interstellar insignias, each minted in solid sterling silver and accentuated with 24-karat gold, including the USS Enterprise Command Insignia, the Klingon Empire Insignia and the Romulan Bird of Prey. Includes a hardwood and glass display case and certificate of authenticity. A new insignia is shipped every other month.

Star Trek: The Next Generation Voice/Character Boxes (PPFD Merchandising, $34.95)—Nine inches high, used as lunch or toy boxes. In three designs—Worf, Ferengi and Borg—each box has a computer chip that allows it to communicate three different phrases.

Star Trek: The Next Generation Coin Banks (Thinkway Toys, $39.99)—Featuring the voice of Brent Spiner, each coin deposit to the **Captain Picard Electronic Model** activates a series of sound and light effects, simulating photon torpedoes, red alert and warp speed. Batteries included. Also available: the nonelectronic Ferengi, Borg and Klingon banks ($19.99).

CLOTHING

Star Trek: The Next Generation Uniforms (Rubie's Costume Co., from $15.99 to $75)—Starfleet uniforms, male and female, in child and adult sizes and various Starfleet colors. Picard, Data, Worf, Geordi and Borg masks also available.

Star Trek: The Next Generation T-Shirts/Sweatshirts (Fine Art Editions, from $20 to $30)—Nine *STNG* designs available, in adult sizes only. Available in either black or white or both, depending on design. A final episode design is also being planned. Also available: sports caps in black, blue or tan ($20).

Star Trek: The Next Generation FX Mugs (Image Design Concepts, $15)— Eleven *STNG* designs available featuring various crew members. Designs change when hot liquid is added to the mugs.

HOLOGRAPHICS

Star Trek: The Next Generation Holographic Collector's Plate (Silverbridge Group Inc., $845)—Limited to 1701 numbered originals, the square "1701-D Orbits Saturn" hologram, designed by *ST* book illustrator Keith Birdsong, comes framed with a certificate of authenticity.

Holograms (A.H. Prismatic, from $2 to $45)—An extensive set of *STNG* hologram products, including stickers, magnets, bookmarks, postcards, prints, key rings, jewelry and hologram boxes.

Holusion Art Print—Romulan Encounter (NVision Grafix Inc., $30)—

One of a series of "holusion" prints (a computer-generated optical illusion, featuring random art patterns that mask three-dimensional objects), this eye-catching experience (50x70 cm) brings the Enterprise face-to-face with a Romulan Warbird.

Star Trek: The Next Generation Photo Plaques (Catch a Star, $260 to $580)—Featuring the photo of a cast member, each plaque is personally autographed.

Star Trek: The Next Generation Commemorative Edition Porcelain Plaque (Samaco Trading Ltd., $95)—Enclosed in wood display case, with built-in easel and hook, the plaque's porcelain surface is adorned by cast and ship. Also available: the **Commemorative Edition USS Enterprise NCC-1701-D Executive Figurine** ($95) and the **Lighted Musical Star Globe Halodome** ($100) featuring the voice of Patrick Stewart and the *STNG* theme.

CATCH A STAR

FAREWELL PARTY

How do you wrap the seven-year run of one of the most successful series in first-run syndication? With a party, of course. On the evening of April 2, 1994—the filming of the final episode having nearly concluded—the cast and crew of *Star Trek: The Next Generation* said farewell in elegant splendor. Here's an inside look at their Hollywood bash, and some tips on making your own *STNG* send-off a smash.

by DONNA WEINERMAN

THE CAST PARTY

DOWN-TO-EARTH ELEGANCE IN HOLLYWOOD

When party organizer Mary Micucci picked up the phone one day in February, the caller on the other end was Paramount. And the studio wanted more than a lasagna-and-salad spread for game show contestants—it was a sparkling concept for the *STNG* wrap party, a concept that would have *nothing* to do with outer space.

"They wanted an evening that everyone would remember," says Micucci, owner of Along Came Mary! catering service. "They wanted something special, something elegant, something different. So the first thing that we did was look for an exciting location."

The final choice: L.A.'s old downtown rail depot, Union Station—a classic of California art deco architecture. "It's a beautiful building that was built in the '30s but has been recently restored," says Micucci. "The party was held in the original ticket concourse, which is now closed to the public and used exclusively for movie shoots and private functions. It's a huge room that could easily hold the 500 invited guests and provide the perfect setting for an elegant event. We even set up bars in the original ticket windows."

Since Paramount wanted a tone of sophistication for the evening, Micucci suggested a color theme of black and white. "The room has 50-foot ceilings and marble floors. All we brought in was up-lighting for the walls and the palm trees. The dance floor was black and white, the tablecloths were black moiré, and the flowers were white. We used beautiful white lilies, roses, tulips and dogwood. The dress was also black and white, or what I'd term 'creative black tie'," added Micucci.

Party Trekkers (clockwise from top left): Patrick Stewart and Avery Brooks. Marina Sirtis and her husband, Michael Lampert. Brent Spiner and his date, Loree McBride along with LeVar Burton and his wife, Stephanie Cozart. Jonathan Frakes and his wife, Genie Francis. Michael Dorn, Marina Sirtis and Brent Spiner. Gates McFadden with her companion, John Talbot.

Micucci also orchestrated the selection of food for the night. "Paramount wanted an international menu, so we set up buffet tables throughout the room with different types of food at each station. There was a wonderful Asian station, an Italian station and a Southwestern station with a huge selection of food. Of course, we had a wide variety of vegetarian items because there generally is a large vegetarian contingent at these parties."

Festivities started at 7 P.M. with hors-d'oeuvres, then dinner at 8 with four "Celebratory Stations": Fiesta Flavors (soft tacos and gourmet quesadillas), Feast from the East (dim sum, spring rolls, crab won ton, vegetable mu shu and firework rice), California Grill (grilled chicken breasts, rosemary bread, eggplant strips, olive bread, gourmet sausages) and Cucina Rustica (pasta and

gourmet pizzas). A fifth station, All-American Sweets, had a wide assortment of desserts, including tiramisu, cookies, wild berry cobbler, fresh fruit and ice cream sundaes. Also shaping the ambience was a versatile jazz group that played low-key instrumentals in the early going, then switched to rock 'n' roll as the night wore on.

For amusement, Paramount also arranged a casino/raffle, where guests gambled with fake money, then turned in their chips in a bid to win a number of prizes. "For this type of party, especially in Hollywood on a Saturday night, you have to create a format for the evening that builds, so that not everything is all at once," Micucci says. "People had a lovely time. They got all decked out. They drank, they ate, they gambled and danced. It was a great send-off for the series."

YOUR PARTY

TAKING YOUR *STNG* SEND-OFF TO THE MAX

We asked professional party planner Ronnie Caplan, head of Michael Caplan Entertainment (Toronto) Inc., how he would make the most of a *STNG* theme party. Here are some of his ideas:

- *Place a giant Federation symbol on the front door to welcome your guests, using cardboard covered in tinfoil.*
- *Tape tinfoil around the TV room and bathroom for a tongue-in-cheek futuristic look.*
- *Pin up life-size posters of STNG characters and alien faces to mirrors throughout your house.*
- *Remove white light bulbs and replace them with colored ones to help achieve a "Transporter Room" look.*
- *Add dry ice to planters and toilets throughout the house (it's inexpensive, but handle with care). Dry ice could also be placed in food or beverage containers and serving platters.*
- *Take unusual objects, spray-paint them silver, and place them on your buffet or display tables. For the centrepiece, use a medley of tinfoil tubes, pipe cleaners, sparkles and confetti, twisty vines or any other oddball items you have around the house.*
- *Experiment with food coloring—for example, make your onion dip red and set it off with blue corn chips.*
- *Serve quirky vegetables and edible flowers.*
- *Label the foods and beverages with Trekker names, like Klingon cola, Starship salad and Data dips.*

EAT LIKE THE CAST AND CREW

We asked Mary Micucci to share her party recipes. The cast and crew enjoyed these at their L.A. wrap party, and they're easy to make—so you'll have them prepared and presented in plenty of time to settle in for the final episode.

··

SOFT TACOS

36-6 in	flour and corn tortillas	36-15cm
6-6 oz	boneless and skinless chicken breasts	6-175 g
1½ lbs	flank steak	750 g

MARINADE

2 cups	olive oil	500 ml
1½ cups	white wine	375 ml
¼ cup	chopped shallots	50 ml
½ bunch	chopped cilantro	½ bunch
2	chiles, finely diced	2
1 tbsp	sweet chili powder	15 ml

Wrap tortillas in foil and heat 10-15 minutes in a 250°F (125°C) oven until warm. (Do this right before serving.) For marinade: Sauté shallots in ½ tbsp (15-25 ml) of oil, then add wine and simmer for 3-5 minutes. Add the rest of the ingredients for the marinade and cool. Marinate meat for 3-4 days and chicken for 1-2 days. Drain meat and barbecue until chicken is done and beef is medium rare. Cut into strips. Serve in warm tortillas with refried black beans, shredded lettuce, assorted salsa, diced tomatoes, grated cheese and onions. Serves 12.

CAJETA CARAMEL SAUCE

qt	goat milk	.95 L
cups	cow's milk	1 L
tsp	cornstarch	3 ml
tsp	baking soda	1 ml
cups	sugar	500 ml

ring goat milk (or cow's milk, if esired) and 3½ cups (875 ml) cow's ilk to a boil. Mix cornstarch, baking oda and ½ cup (125 ml) cow's milk. dd to first mixture and bring to a boil. ake 1½ cups (375 ml) sugar and gradally stir into milk mixture until disolved. Continue cooking. Take 1½ ups (375 ml) sugar, cook in frying pan ver low heat and caramelize till light olden brown. Then add other mixture lowly. It may foam up. Continue boilng until it begins to thicken (about 30-

50 minutes). Lower heat and continue to cook, stirring constantly, until it forms a thread and coats a wooden spoon.

CAJETA CARAMEL SUNDAES

3 cups	Cajeta Caramel Sauce	750 ml
2-3 qts	vanilla ice cream	1.89-2.84 L
2 cups	whipped cream	500 ml
1 tsp	ground cinnamon	5 ml
3 cups	hot fudge sauce	750 ml
	(if desired)	
½-¾ lb	toasted pine nuts	250-375 g

To assemble sundaes: Place scoop of ice cream in dish. Add Caramel Sauce and hot fudge sauce (if desired). Top with whipped cream and ground cinnamon. Sprinkle top with toasted pine nuts. Serves 12.

Well, we never could keep a secret. After months of speculation, Trekkers everywhere are dying for a sneak peek at the series finale, the *STNG* feature movie (with the working title of "Star Trek: Generations") to be released in November, and the next series, *Star Trek: Voyager*, which will make its debut in January 1995. And while we won't tell you everything, we *will* tell you just enough to whet your appetite.

by MICHAEL LOGAN

THE SERIES FINALE

In "Encounter at Farpoint"—*STNG*'s pilot episode—the command crew of the USS Enterprise was hijacked and sentenced to death in a kangaroo court by the Q, an omnipotent super-race that considered humanity too barbarous to proceed any further.

"In an effort to bring things full circle with the series finale, we are again exploring the concept of mankind being put on trial," (right) says executive producer Rick Berman. "We wanted a nice bookend." Returning to raise hell as Q is the popular John de Lancie and—to further delight fans—Berman will also bring back Colm Meaney as O'Brien (now seen on *DS9*) and Denise Crosby as Tasha Yar (the starship security chief who was killed by the alien Armus in the first season's "Skin of Evil").

"We wanted to end with a story of sweeping quality and one that embodies the themes that have made *Star Trek* important to us," Berman continues. Written by Brannon Braga and Ronald D. Moore (who also penned the upcoming movie "Star Trek: Generations"), the two-hour "All Good Things..." will find Picard and crew in the past, present and future.

"We haven't taken every single loose thread over seven years and tied it up, because hopefully there will be a whole series of movies to take care of those," notes Berman. "But there is a very strong sense of finality to the episode. It's not morose. We don't kill anybody or make any catastrophic changes to the series structure, and it doesn't interfere with the continuation of the characters in the movie, but there is completion. Riker will not wake up in the shower and tell us it's all been a dream. We owe that to the audience."

THE NEXT SERIES

Just as *Deep Space Nine* allowed Gene Roddenberry's successors to explore issues of darkness and conflict that didn't quite fit into the sunny *STNG*, a third series spinoff, *Star Trek: Voyager*, promises to explore new horizons its predecessors haven't. Debuting in January 1995 as the cornerstone of Paramount's new broadcast network, *Voyager* is created and executive produced by Michael Piller, Jeri Taylor and the man who would be Gene—Rick Berman.

"Though *Voyager* will, like *Next Generation*, be a ship-based show, it'll have many fresh elements that will allow us to do things we've never done before," says Berman, who has overseen the *Trek* franchise since Roddenberry bowed out after *STNG*'s first season. Though *Voyager*'s 24th-century time frame—contemporary to *STNG* and *DS9*—will allow for the occasional crossover guest, the crew of this Starship (unlike the Enterprise)

will be a hybrid of bonafide Starfleet officers and former members of a vigilante organization known as the Maquis. Notes Berman, "It'll be the joining together of two ships one-to-one in an effort to accomplish a common goal." Though Berman declines comment, that goal, reportedly, is to find their way back home after being transported 70 years into their future. Berman is also mum about rumors that *Voyager* will break with *Trek* tradition and have a female captain. But he *will* offer up these tasty tidbits:

"*Voyager*'s cast of regulars will include a female half-Klingon, half-human who is embarrassed about her heritage. We'll have a Vulcan on the show—something we've never had on any series since the original. There will be two characters from a species we've never seen before. We will also have a native American. He'll be a member of a tribe of Indians who left Earth some time in the 22nd century to establish a colony where they could more closely relate to their cultural identity. He was born and raised on one of these colonies but went back to Earth to become a Starfleet officer." Casting will commence in June.

While Paramount's enthusiasm for *Voyager* is running high, Berman is well aware of a potential backlash from unhappy *Trekkers*. After all, *DS9*—which was warmly welcomed—wasn't replacing the beloved *STNG*. But *Voyager* is.

"I can really relate to that feeling,"

concedes Berman. "I'm going to miss *The Next Generation*. I will mourn its exit as much as the fans will—but I am not responsible for taking it off the air. Besides, *Voyager* is not a replacement as far as we are concerned. It is the next step. It's not as if we're killing your baby sister and adopting a new kid and bringing him home. *Voyager* will have twists and turns that will make it a very unique show. It will stand on its own—and we're very excited about it."

THE MOVIE—STAR TREK: GENERATIONS

Though the motion picture "Star Trek: Generations" will bring together the 23rd century's Capt. James T. Kirk and the 24th century's Capt. Jean-Luc Picard, executive producer Rick Berman insists the flick features "no time travel whatsoever." Hey, c'mon. We all know the two series were separated by some 85 years! But Berman isn't coughing up details on how this celestial convergence occurs. Nor will he discuss the rampant rumors that Kirk—to be played once again by William Shatner—is going to die. (Ooops, too late! Actor Malcolm McDowell, cast as the film's villain, Dr. Saran, has already been quoted in Daily Variety as saying, "I get to kill Kirk.") Another verboten topic: Whoopi Goldberg. Not only is Berman under gag order not to discuss her involvement in the film, but Paramount doesn't mention her in press releases, either. But rest assured that Goldberg—as Guinan—will definitely be on board (a studio spy tells us, "Whoopi has a great role but doesn't want to be mentioned in the advertisements or credits").

Confirmed for the film are all seven leads in *STNG* and, from the classic cast, Walter Koenig (Chekov) and James Doohan (Scotty). According to Berman, there was no room for Nichelle Nichols (Uhura) or George Takei (Sulu), but DeForest Kelley (Bones) and Leonard Nimoy (Spock) were offered roles and declined.

Directed by David Carson (who helmed the première of *DS9*), movie No. 7 is filming off the coast of Southern California and in the Valley of Fire, a Nevada state park known for its spectacular rock formations. But any Trekker truly anxious for more details should start hounding those sci-fi gatherings. Huffs Berman, "A week after it was written, we found a copy of the movie script for sale at a *Trek* convention."

SYNOPSIS GUIDE

Over the course of its seven years, the Galaxy-class USS Enterprise NCC-1701-D, under the command of Capt. Jean-Luc Picard, has logged some 178 hours of adventure, intrigue and romance—not to mention space exploration. Now, as the Enterprise departs the small screen to resume its mission at a theatre near you, TV GUIDE presents our complete log of its voyages.

On the following pages, organized by season and in order of air date, you'll find a description for each *STNG* episode ever filmed. These are the current TV GUIDE descriptions—expanded to include additional cast information, title, stardate and production number (the sequence in which episodes were filmed). For noteworthy episodes—ones that introduced new characters, explained historical events, featured prominent guest stars or simply delivered superior entertainment—we've included our critical commentary, published here for the first time.

 And, with your help, we've chosen 30 episodes as our all-time favorites. Rankings, from 1 to 30, are based on our opinion and on those of TV GUIDE readers—who nominated their favorite episodes in our "Great Debate" survey, conducted at the end of the sixth season. These all-time favorite episodes are illustrated by means of an *STNG* communicator badge (left) and a number to indicate the episode's overall rank. Two-part episodes are counted as one, and thus receive the same rank.

A WORD ABOUT STARDATES

A stardate is the universal time calculation used by the United Federation of Planets and introduced to the classic *Trek* by series creator Gene Roddenberry—who borrowed the notion from the Julian date currently used by astronomers. Created by Julius Caesar, that time calculation measures the number of days elapsed since Jan. 1, 4713 B.C.: exactly 2,449,496 days as of May 23, 1994, the release date of *STNG*'s final episode. Astronomers use only the last four digits—making 9496 the Julian date for May 23, 1994. A single digit, from 0 to 9, following a decimal point is added to represent one of 10 time increments for each 24-hour period.

In the classic *Trek*, the four-digit Julian date was renamed "stardate." But rather than serving as a precise measurement of each episode's time frame, it was simply used as a reminder that the series was set in the future. To distinguish *STNG*'s stardates from those of its predecessor, Roddenberry introduced a fifth digit. While still not a precise measurement of each episode's time frame, attentive viewers *will* notice somewhat of a pattern (right).

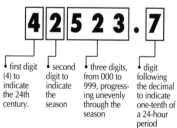

first digit (4) to indicate the 24th century.

second digit to indicate the season

three digits, from 000 to 999, progressing unevenly through the season

digit following the decimal to indicate one-tenth of a 24-hour period

First Season

In what was perhaps the most anticipated series première of all time, *Star Trek: The Next Generation* began its syndicated run the week of Sept. 28, 1987, with the two-hour pilot episode "Encounter at Farpoint," and was seen by more than 12 million North American households. Set in the 24th century, some 85 years after the classic *Trek*, the further voyages of the Starship Enterprise took up the continuing mission "to boldly go where no one has gone before." Outfitted with a host of new devices, including a holodeck, the new USS Enterprise (NCC 1701-D)—a first-of-its-kind, Galaxy-class starship—and its crew of over 1000 were off to a promising start. Despite early criticism of plot lines that too closely resembled those of the original, *STNG* quickly developed its own devoted following and steadily climbed in both ratings and in the number of stations airing the program in prime time—a first for a syndicated series. By year's end, the series had become the No. 1 first-run hourlong series in syndication, reaching 9.4 million people in the U.S. and giving Paramount the confidence to boost *STNG*'s budget to $1.5 million US per episode. In Canada, stations in virtually every market had picked up the series, proving that North American Trekkers were once again hooked on the continuing adventures of a universe that just wouldn't die.

ENCOUNTER AT FARPOINT
Week of Sept. 28, 1987, No. 721
STARDATE: 41153.7

In the series pilot, Capt. Jean-Luc Picard (Patrick Stewart) meets the crew of the new Starship Enterprise and embarks on his first mission: to visit the Farpoint station on the planet Deneb IV. But before reaching their destination, the explorers are captured by the alien life form Q. **Groppler Zorn:** Michael Bell. **Lieut. Torres:** Jimmy Ortega.

[Providing a sentimental link to the classic Star Trek, DeForest Kelley (right) appears as the irascible Admiral Leonard McCoy, now 137 years old and still hating to beam aboard. The pilot episode establishes how some of the crew meet and hints at their backgrounds. And in what was to become a recurring role, John de Lancie steals the show as the mischievous alien Q. Watch for Colm Meaney (later Miles O'Brien) as the conn ensign with no name. The pilot first ran as a two-hour program but is repeated in two one-hour segments (Nos. 101, 102).]

THE NAKED NOW
Week of Oct. 5, 1987, No. 103
STARDATE: 41209.2
While investigating mysterious deaths aboard another starship, Geordi (LeVar Burton) becomes infected with a mind-altering illness that spreads to the rest of the Enterprise crew. **Chief Engineer Sarah MacDougal:** Brooke Bundy. **Assistant Engineer Jim Shimoda:** Benjamin W.S. Lum. **Transporter Chief:** Michael Rider.

[A tribute of sorts, the first regular STNG episode borrows its plot from the classic Trek *episode "The Naked Time," and identifies its medical crisis by pulling up the log of the Federation's first USS* Enterprise, *captained by James T. Kirk.* **Best scene:** *The unexpected romantic encounter between hot-blooded security chief Tasha Yar and Lt.-Cmdr. Data, in which the android explains that he is "fully functional. In every way, of course. I am programmed in multiple techniques, a broad variety of pleasing."]*

CODE OF HONOR
Week of Oct. 12, 1987, No. 104
STARDATE: 41235.25
While the crew is stationed on the planet Ligon II, the inhabitants abduct Tasha and force Picard to abide by their code of honor to obtain her release. **Lutan:** Jessie Lawrence Ferguson. **Yareena:** Karole Selmon. **Hagon:** James Louis Watkins. **Transporter Chief:** Michael Rider.

THE LAST OUTPOST
Week of Oct. 19, 1987, No. 107
STARDATE: 41386.4
Picard (Patrick Stewart) suspects that the hostile Ferengi are responsible for a sudden energy loss that immobilizes the Enterprise. **Letek:** Armin Shimerman. **Mordoc:** Jake Dengel. **Kayron:** Tracey Walter. **Portal:** Darryl Henriques. **DaiMon Taar:** Mike Gomez.

[First appearance of the Ferengi, super-capitalists of the galaxy. Watch for Armin Shimerman (later Quark on DS9) in his first of three Ferengi roles.]

WHERE NO ONE HAS GONE BEFORE
Week of Oct. 26, 1987, No. 106
STARDATE: 41263.1
A glitch in the Enterprise's propulsion system catapults the starship into a galaxy where mental powers become extraordinary, and the crew find that they are what they think. **Kosinski:** Stanley Kamel. **Traveler:** Eric Menyuk. **Yvette Gessard Picard:** Herta Ware. **Lt.-Cmdr. Argyle:** Biff Yeager. **Crew Member:** Charles Dayton. **Ballerina:** Victoria Dillard.

[First glimpse of the late Jack Crusher appearing as an image to both his widow Beverly and to Picard. And son Wesley Crusher is accorded the rank of acting ensign by the captain. First appearance of the Traveler, who hints at Wesley's true destiny, to be resolved in the seventh season's "Journey's End."]

LONELY AMONG US
Week of Nov. 2, 1987, No. 108
STARDATE: 41249.3
While escorting aliens to the planet Parliament, a UFP diplomatic outpost, Picard (Patrick Stewart) and his crew are enveloped by a cloud that seizes control of their minds and alters their behavior. **Ssestar:** John Durbin. **First Security Guard:** Colm Meaney. **Lt.-Cmdr. Singh:** Kavi Raz.

[First hint of Data's fascination with the fictional Sherlock Holmes, as the android adopts the methods of the legendary detective to solve a number of puzzling ship malfunctions.]

JUSTICE
Week of Nov. 9, 1987, No. 109
STARDATE: 41255.6
Plans for a vacation on the paradisiacal

Rubicam Three are disrupted when Wesley (Wil Wheaton) breaks a planetary law; meanwhile, a hostile vessel objecting to human colonization confronts the Enterprise. **Rivan:** Brenda Bakke. **Liator:** Jay Louden.

[First-rate confrontation between Picard and Dr. Crusher, who urges the captain to violate the Prime Directive to save her son. Reluctantly, he does.]

THE BATTLE
Week of Nov. 16, 1987, No. 110
STARDATE: 41723.9
A former Starfleet vessel now belonging to the Ferengi leader Bok (Frank Corsentino) is returned to Picard—complete with a mind-altering apparatus. **Kazago:** Doug Warhit. **Rata:** Robert Towers.

[This episode explores the Battle of Maxia in which Picard, then in command of the USS Stargazer, used the famous "Picard Manoeuvre" to defeat the Ferengi. With vengeance on his mind, Bok would return in the seventh season's "Bloodlines."]

HIDE AND Q
Week of Nov. 23, 1987, No. 111
STARDATE: 41590.5
The Enterprise crew meet up with the enigmatic Q (John de Lancie), who forces them to participate in a deadly game that pits the players against fanged creatures.

[Q, in his second appearance, tempts Riker with the powers of the Q—and in turn, Riker tempts his crewmates with the "gifts" his powers can provide.]

HAVEN
Week of Nov. 30, 1987, No. 105
STARDATE: 41294.5
Deanna's mother, Lwaxana Troi (Majel Barrett), shows up with news of an impending wedding—the prearranged marriage of Deanna and the son (Rob Knepper) of an old family friend. **Wyatt**

Miller: Rob Knepper. **Victoria Miller:** Nan Martin. **Steven Miller:** Robert Ellenstein. **Mr. Homn:** Carel Struycken. **Valeda Innis:** Anna Katarina. **Wrenn:** Raye Birk. **Ariana:** Danitza Kingsley.

[Majel Barrett—Nurse Chapel of the classic Trek and Gene Roddenberry's wife in real life—has her first of a series of scene-stealing appearances as Deanna's mother, the flirtatious Lwaxana Troi, the one individual able to make the even-tempered Deanna lose her cool. Watch for Carel Struycken (Lurch in "The Addams Family") as Mr. Homn.]

THE BIG GOODBYE
Week of Jan. 11, 1988, No. 113
STARDATE: 41997.7
In this Peabody Award-winning episode, Picard, Crusher and Data re-create 1941 San Francisco via the holodeck, but when the system malfunctions, they find themselves at bay in the 20th century. **Cyrus Redblock:** Lawrence Tierney. **Felix Leech:** Harvey Jason. **Lieut. Dan Bell:** William Boyett. **Whalen:** David Selburg. **Lieut. McNary:** Gary Armagnal.

[First appearance of Picard as his favorite holodeck character, Dixon Hill, a 1940s hard-boiled private eye from Amazing Detective Stories magazine. Best scene: Like Kirk, who often came up with novel excuses to explain Spock's ears, Picard explains Data's skin tone with an ingenious "He's from South America."]

DATALORE
Week of Jan. 18, 1988, No. 114
STARDATE: 41242.4
While exploring Data's home planet, the

crew discovers a collection of body parts, which, when assembled, create an android that's a dead ringer for Data (Brent Spiner). **Lt.-Cmdr. Argyle:** Biff Yeager.

[Brent Spiner shines in a double role when, in the first of several encounters, Data meets his evil twin brother, Lore—Dr. Noonian Soong's earlier, but unsuspected, attempt at the ultimate android.]

ANGEL ONE
Week of Jan. 25, 1988, No. 115
STARDATE: 41636.9
On the female-dominated planet Angel One, the crew discovers that the survivors of a Federation freighter accident are now fugitives because they oppose the matriarchy. **Beata:** Karen Montgomery. **Ramsey:** Sam Hennings. **Ariel:** Patricia McPherson. **Trent:** Leonard John Crowfoot.

11001001
Week of Feb. 1, 1988, No. 116
STARDATE: 41365.9
When the computer indicates a pending disaster, the crew evacuates the Enterprise, unaware that members of a computer-dependent species have sabotaged the ship's software. **Minuet:** Carolyn McCormick. **Cmdr. Orfil Quinteros:** Gene Dynarski. **Piano Player:** Jack Sheldon.

[In the third episode featuring the holodeck—one of STNG's cleverest devices and a fan favorite—Jonathan Frakes gets to show off his real-life trombone-playing skills while a holodeck program that's been tampered with tempts Riker with his fantasy mate. And Data takes up painting to experience human forms of expression.]

TOO SHORT A SEASON
Week of Feb. 8, 1988, No. 112
STARDATE: 41309.5
The Enterprise transports Admiral Mark

Jameson (Clayton Rohner), a renowned but ailing negotiator, to Mordan IV to mediate in a hostage crisis instigated by that planet's governor, Karnas (Michael Pataki). **Anne Jameson:** Marsha Hunt.

[Watch for Michael Pataki, who appeared as the Klingon, Korax, in the classic Trek's "The Trouble With Tribbles."]

WHEN THE BOUGH BREAKS
Week of Feb. 15, 1988, No. 118
STARDATE: 41509.1
The technologically advanced but sterile race of the planet Aldea decide to remedy their plight by kidnapping children from the Enterprise—including Wesley (Wil Wheaton). **Radue:** Jerry Hardin. **Rashella:** Brenda Strong. **Katie:** Jandi Swanson. **Melian:** Paul Lambert. **Duana:** Ivy Bethune.

HOME SOIL
Week of Feb. 22, 1988, No. 117
STARDATE: 41463.9
While visiting Velara III, where terraformers labor to make the barren planet more habitable, the crew is mystified by a bizarre accident that claims the life of one of the workers. **Kurt Mandl:** Walter Gotell. **Louisa Kim:** Elizabeth Lindsey. **Bjorn Benson:** Gerard Prendergast. **Arthur Malencon:** Mario Roccuzzo.

*[Inspiration for this plot line is owed to an episode from the classic Trek titled "Devil in the Dark." **Best line:** "Ugly bags of mostly water," the Velarans' term for humans.]*

COMING OF AGE
Week of March 14, 1988, No. 119
STARDATE: 41416.2
Wesley (Wil Wheaton) takes the Starfleet entrance exam, while Picard's performance as a commander is evaluated. **Admiral Gregory Quinn:** Ward Costello. **Lt.-Cmdr. Dexter Remmick:** Robert Schenkkan. **Mordock:** John Putch. **Tac Officer Chang:** Robert Ito. **Jake Kurland:**

Stephen Gregory. **T'Shanik:** Tasia Valenza. **Oliana Mirren:** Estee Chandler. **Rondon:** Robert Riordan.

[First STNG Vulcan in a speaking role. Picard turns down the rank of admiral and the position of commandant of Starfleet Academy to stay aboard the Enterprise.]

HEART OF GLORY
Week of March 21, 1988, No. 120
STARDATE: 41503.7
Worf (Michael Dorn) finds himself torn between two leaders when he learns that fugitive Klingons rescued by the Enterprise are plotting to reestablish their warrior race and want Worf to join their side. **Cmdr. Korris:** Vaughn Armstrong. **Lieut. Konmel:** Charles H. Hyman. **K'nera:** David Froman. **Kunivas:** Robert Bauer. **Ramos:** Dennis Madalone.

[Explored more fully in a series of later episodes, Worf's background is introduced, and we are brought up to date on the state of the Klingon-Federation relationship. The Klingon dialogue is the last to be spoken prior to the introduction of the Klingon language as developed by linguist Marc Okrand. For information on "The Klingon Dictionary," see page 52.]

THE ARSENAL OF FREEDOM
Week of April 11, 1988, No. 121
STARDATE: 41798.2
While the Enterprise crew searches for a missing spacecraft on the planet Minos, site of a lost civilization, Picard and Crusher (Patrick Stewart, Gates McFadden) disappear. **The Peddler:** Vincent Schiavelli. **Capt. Paul Rice:** Marco Rodriguez. **Chief Engineer Logan:** Vyto Ruginis. **Ensign Lian T'Su:** Julia Nickson. **Lieut. (Junior Grade) Orfil Solis:** George de la Pena.

[Fast-moving episode in which Picard must tend to the wounded Dr. Crusher and we learn more about Beverly's background. Best line: Riker telling the holographic image of the USS Drake's Capt. Rice—Riker's friend and former Starfleet classmate—that he's from "a good ship," the USS Lollipop.]

SYMBIOSIS
Week of April 18, 1988, No. 123
STARDATE: Unknown
When the Enterprise carries out a mission of mercy, Picard (Patrick Stewart) becomes embroiled in a bitter trade dispute between neighboring planets. **Sobi:** Judson Scott. **T'Jon:** Merritt Butrick. **Romas:** Richard Lineback. **Langor:** Kimberly Farr.

[In this episode, the issue of drug addiction gets the subtle treatment as the planets Brekka and Ornara battle over the drug felecium—a drug grown only on Brekka and required to cure a 200-year-old Ornaran plague. Watch for two "Star Trek II: The Wrath of Khan" actors in guest appearances—the late Merritt Butrick, remembered as Kirk's son, David Marcus, and Judson Scott, who played one of Khan's followers.]

SKIN OF EVIL
Week of April 25, 1988, No. 122
STARDATE: 41601.3
After crashing the shuttlecraft on to Vagra II, Troi (Marina Sirtis) is held hostage by a sadistic creature that delights in taunting the rescue team. **Armus:** Mart McChesney. **Asst. Chief Engineer Leland Lynch:** Walker Boone. **Nurse:** Brad Zerbst. **Lieut. Ben Prieto:** Raymond Forchion.

[A real Star Trek first: The death of a major character, security chief Tasha Yar (opposite), who was written out of the series at the request of actress Denise Crosby. A moving episode for the actors and characters alike. Crosby would return in a series of later episodes, however—as Yar in the third season's "Yesterday's Enterprise," and as Tasha's daughter, Romulan Cmdr. Sela, in the two-part episodes "Redemption" and "Unification," and again as Yar in the final episode "All Good Things..."]

WE'LL ALWAYS HAVE PARIS
Week of May 2, 1988, No. 124
STARDATE: 41697.9
Picard is reunited with his first love, Jenice Manheim (Michelle Phillips), when the Enterprise rescues her husband, a scientist who breaks into another dimension while conducting time experiments. **Dr. Paul Manheim:** Rod Loomis. **Gabrielle:** Isabel Lorca. **Lieut. Dean:** Dan Kern. **Edouard:** Jean-Paul Vignon. **Transporter Chief Herbert:** Lance Spellerberg.

[The first appearance of a major guest star, Michelle Phillips (with Patrick Stewart, above), a fan of the original Trek. She never quite clicked as Picard's long-lost love, but the episode does serve to humanize Picard and hint at Dr. Crusher's true feelings for the duty-bound captain.]

CONSPIRACY
Week of May 9, 1988, No. 125
STARDATE: 41775.5
Picard (Patrick Stewart) investigates a plot to infiltrate the highest level of the Starfleet command and returns to Earth to confront the conspirators. **Admiral Savar:** Henry Darrow. **Admiral Quinn:** Ward Costello. **Lt.-Cmdr. Dexter Remmick:** Robert Schenkkan. **Admiral Aaron:** Ray Reinhardt. **Capt. Walker Keel:** Jonathan Farwell. **Capt. Rixx:** Michael Berryman. **Capt. Tryla Scott:** Ursaline Bryant.

[One of the goriest STNG episodes ever filmed, with its scenes of death and worm-eating. Watch for Henry Darrow as the first Vulcan on STNG to deliver the legendary Vulcan Nerve Pinch.]

THE NEUTRAL ZONE
Week of May 16, 1988, No. 126
STARDATE: 41986.0
The crew discovers three cryogenically preserved bodies on a 20th-century Earth satellite just as the Enterprise is ordered to the Neutral Zone to confront hostile Romulans. **Cmdr. T-Bok:** Marc Alaimo. **Sub-Cmdr. Thei:** Anthony James. **L.Q. "Sonny" Clemonds:** Leon Rippy. **Clare Raymond:** Gracie Harrison. **Ralph Offenhouse:** Peter Mark Richman.

[The Federation's first contact with the Romulans in 53 years. And we finally learn that the current Earth year is 2364.]

ENCOUNTERS
PLANETS: Aldea, Angel One, Deneb IV, Ligon II, Minos, Mordan IV, Omicron Theta, Relva 7, Rubicam Three, Styris IV, Vagra II, Velara III, Sarona VII, Vandor IX
RACES: Aldeans, Anticans, Bandi, Brekkians, Bynars, Edo, Ferengi, Jarada, Klingons, Ligonians, Ornarans, The Q, Romulans, Tarellians, Vulcans
SHIPS: Ajax, Drake, Charleston, Stargazer, Tsiolkovsky

Second Season

As the second season began, numerous changes were on the boards for characters and cast alike. Most notable is the absence of Dr. Beverly Crusher, who, having accepted a posting at Starfleet Medical, has been replaced by Dr. Kate Pulaski (Diana Muldaur, a guest star on the classic *Trek*)—whose sometimes crusty and stubborn personality is reminiscent of that other famous doctor in classic *Trek* history. Among the crew, La Forge becomes chief engineer, while Worf's promotion to security chief (replacing the late Tasha Yar) is made permanent. Meanwhile, Riker has grown a beard and Deanna adopts a more flattering hairstyle and uniform. Also joining the Enterprise, to assume bartending duties in the ship's Ten Forward lounge, is Picard's old friend and new recruit, Guinan (played by Whoopi Goldberg), who, like most bartenders, serves up good advice with the synthehol. And while ambitious plot lines would give way this year to character development and a chance for the cast to have some fun, the 1988 strike by the Writers' Guild delayed the start of the season and shortened its run from the planned 26 episodes to 22—the quality and insight of which, however, gave viewers a much more complete view of the Federation in the 24th century.

THE CHILD
Week of Nov. 21, 1988, No. 127
STARDATE: 42073.1
As the crew rushes samples of a disease organism to a research station, Troi (Marina Sirtis) announces that she's pregnant. Whoopi Goldberg joins the cast as Guinan. **Lt.-Cmdr. Hester Dealt:** Seymour Cassel. **Ian Andrew Troi:** R.J. Williams. **Transporter Chief:** Colm Meaney. **Miss Glad-stone:** Dawn Arnemann. **Young Ian:** Zachary Benjamin.

[In this episode, we learn of Troi's attachment to her human father, Ian Andrew— whom we meet in the seventh season's "Dark Page," and in whose memory Troi names her child—and gain insight into her character when she stubbornly refuses to give up her alien baby. Wesley also undergoes some character definition as he ponders, but decides against, joining his mother at Starfleet Medical.]

WHERE SILENCE HAS LEASE
Week of Nov. 28, 1988, No. 128
STARDATE: 42193.6
En route to the Morgana Quadrant, the Enterprise is trapped in an inexplicable void, where the crew discovers a deserted spacecraft. **Nagilum:** Earl Boen. **Ensign Haskell:** Charles Douglass. **Transporter Chief:** Colm Meaney.

[First glimpse of Worf's holodeck-enhanced Klingon exercise program.]

ELEMENTARY, DEAR DATA
Week of Dec. 5, 1988, No. 129
STARDATE: 42286.3
When the crew gets a few days off, Geordi (LeVar Burton) plans a diversion for himself and Data on the holodeck—they play Watson and Holmes in Victorian England (above). **Moriarty:** Daniel Davis. **Lestrade:** Alan Shearman. **Engineer Clancy:** Anne Ramsay.

[The title says it all in this light-hearted episode that brings to mind some of the best aspects of the classic Trek. Here, the plot takes a back seat to comedy and the interplay between characters, as Data struggles to develop a sense of humor and learn how to tell a joke—aided and abetted by Saturday Night Live comedian Joe Piscopo (below) doing an excellent impression of a toothy Jerry Lewis. And in pre-fame roles are William O. Campbell ("The Rocketeer") and Teri Hatcher (Lois & Clark).]

[Wonderfully written episode linking Data's fascination with Sherlock Holmes to his ongoing quest to become human. The episode presents the android with the opportunity to display some truly human characteristics, such as loyalty to his friends, and adds the strange obsession with his Holmesian pipe. Begins the debate over the nature of a sentient being—in this case, the holodeck-generated Professor Moriarty—a debate that will be rekindled in "The Measure of a Man," a subsequent second-season episode. Professor Moriarty, meanwhile, would return in the sixth season's "Ship in a Bottle." Watch for Anne Ramsay (Mad About You) in a small role.]

THE OUTRAGEOUS OKONA
Week of Dec. 12, 1988, No. 130
STARDATE: 42402.7
The crew hosts the captain of a disabled ship, a charming rogue who's accused of philandering and jewel theft; meanwhile, Data tries to understand humor. **Capt. Thadiun Okona:** William O. Campbell. **Debin:** Douglas Rowe. **Kushell:** Albert Stratton. **Yanar:** Rosalind Ingledew. **Benzan:** Kieran Mulroney. **Lieut. B.G. Robinson:** Teri Hatcher. **The Comic:** Joe Piscopo. **Guinan:** Whoopi Goldberg.

LOUD AS A WHISPER
Week of Jan. 9, 1989, No. 132
STARDATE: 42477.2
A deaf war mediator (Howie Seago) is escorted by the Away Team to the site of a centuries-long conflict. **Warrior/Adonis:** Leo Damian. **Woman:** Marnie Mosiman. **Scholar:** Thomas Oglesby. **Transporter Chief:** Colm Meaney.

[Interesting insight into how the 24th century approaches physical disabilities. Geordi ponders—but ultimately turns down—Dr. Pulaski's offer to restore his sight surgically, while mediator Riva (Howie Seago, who is deaf in real life) uses deafness to his advantage in mediating an end to the conflict.]

THE SCHIZOID MAN
Week of Jan. 23, 1989, No. 131
STARDATE: 42437.5
The Away Team, led by Data, goes on a mission of mercy to help a dying scientist (W. Morgan Sheppard) whose final act causes the android to suffer a split personality. **Lieut. Selar:** Suzie Plakson. **Kareen Brianon:** Barbara Alyn Woods.

[Data meets Dr. Ira Graves, the man who mentored his creator and who— by implanting himself in Data's mind —ultimately teaches him more about the human condition. And watch for for him to try out a Riker-inspired beard. Suzie Plakson (Love & War) makes her first appearance here as the Vulcan Lieut. Selar, and also appears later in the season as Worf's Klingon mate, K'Ehleyr.]

UNNATURAL SELECTION
Week of Jan. 30, 1989, No. 133
STARDATE: 42494.8
Responding to an emergency call for help from a supply ship, the Enterprise encounters an epidemic that causes rapid aging and death. **Dr. Sara Kingsley:** Patricia Smith. **Transporter Chief:** Colm Meaney. **Capt. Taggert:** J. Patrick McNamara.

[Another tribute to the classic series, this episode borrows the essence of its plot from "The Deadly Years," while providing a more intriguing technological solution to the aging epidemic. Dr. Pulaski's first central role.]

A MATTER OF HONOR
Week of Feb. 6, 1989, No. 134
STARDATE: 42506.5
An exchange program that allows Cmdr. Riker (Jonathan Frakes) to become the first Federation officer to serve on a Klingon vessel turns into a dangerous confrontation between the Klingons and the Enterprise over an outbreak of starship-eroding bacteria. **Ensign Mendon:** John Putch. **Capt. Kargan:** Christopher Collins. **Klag:** Brian Thompson. **Transporter Chief:** Colm Meaney. **Tactics Officer:** Peter Parros. **Vekma:** Laura Drake.

[Solid drama depicting Klingon culture and values. Jonathan Frakes shines in a role in which Riker must prove his toughness in the eyes of his Klingon hosts—and manages to do so when he bullies the Enterprise into surrender. Colm Meaney's character, Transporter Chief O'Brien, finally gets a last name.]

THE MEASURE OF A MAN
Week of Feb. 13, 1989, No. 135
STARDATE: 42523.7
The officer in charge of a new starbase orders Data to be disassembled for study. When Data refuses, a judge advocate general (Amanda McBroom) sets up a hearing with Picard as defense counsel and Riker as prosecutor. **Capt. Phillipa Louvois:** Amanda McBroom. **Admiral Nakamura:** Clyde Kusatsu. **Cmdr. Bruce Maddox:** Brian Brophy. **O'Brien:** Colm Meaney. **Guinan:** Whoopi Goldberg.

[Picking up a theme explored earlier in "Elementary, Dear Data," Data's rights as a sentient being are put to the test. Best scene: Riker, as prosecutor, offers proof that Data is only a machine— by switching him off. Also a first glimpse of the officers' weekly poker game, later to become a recurring plot device.]

THE DAUPHIN
Week of Feb. 20, 1989, No. 136
STARDATE: 42568.8
When the Enterprise is assigned to escort a young woman (Jaime Hubbard) to Daled Four, her overprotective guardian (Paddi Edwards) tries to keep the lovesick Wesley at bay. **Anya:** Paddi Edwards. **O'Brien:** Colm Meaney. **Anya as Girl:** Madchen Amick. **Anya as Animal:** Cindy Sorenson. **Ensign Gibson:** Jennifer Barlow.

[Wesley suffers through his first romance with the allasomorph Salia, and has some rather adult decisions to make after he finds out about her true shape-changing nature. The notion of a shape-changing being was later to be refined on DS9 in the person of shape-shifter Odo (Rene Auberjonois). Look for Madchen Amick, later seen on Twin Peaks.]

CONTAGION
Week of March 20, 1989, No. 137
STARDATE: 42609.1
When a computer virus renders the Enterprise vulnerable to Romulan attack in the Neutral Zone, Picard and the Away Team beam down to the site of a lost civilization to find the source of the infection. **Capt. Donald Varley:** Thalmus Rasulala. **Sub-Cmdr. Taris:** Carolyn Seymour. **O'Brien:** Colm Meaney.

THE ROYALE
Week of March 27, 1989, No. 138
STARDATE: 42625.4
Hunting for clues about the wreckage of an Air Force ship, the Away Team lands in the Hotel Royale, where Riker, Worf and Data are cut off from the Enterprise and can find no exit. **Texas:** Noble Willingham. **Asst. Manager:** Sam Anderson. **Vanessa:** Jill Jacobson. **The Bell Boy:** Leo Garcia. **O'Brien:** Colm Meaney. **Mickey D:** Gregory Beecroft.

TIME SQUARED
Week of April 3, 1989, No. 139
STARDATE: 42679.2
The Enterprise encounters a shuttlecraft with an unconscious double of Capt. Picard on board. **O'Brien:** Colm Meaney.

*[Suspenseful time-travel tale featuring Patrick Stewart in a dual role as Picard now, and six hours in the future. **Best scene:** The captain shoots his future self to keep that Picard from abandoning the Enterprise.]*

THE ICARUS FACTOR
Week of April 24, 1989, No. 140
STARDATE: 42686.4
When Riker is offered the captaincy of a starship, his delight turns to hostility when the officer assigned to brief him turns out to be his estranged father. Meanwhile, Worf suffers a spiritual crisis which Data, Geordi and Wesley attempt to remedy by means of the holodeck. **O'Brien:** Colm Meaney. **Kyle Riker:** Mitchell Ryan. **Transporter Operator Herbert:** Lance Spellerberg.

[Both Riker and Worf come to terms with the past: Riker with his father's abandonment of him at the age of 15; and Worf with his Klingon heritage. For the second time, Riker will turn down a captaincy to stay aboard the Enterprise. We also learn something of Dr. Pulaski's much-married past and her affair with Riker's father. But the best is kept for last: a glimpse of the

challenging Klingon Age of Ascension rite as re-created via the holodeck. Try spotting Entertainment Tonight *anchor John Tesh in a cameo as a one of Worf's Ascension Chamber tormentors. Hint: He's the one on the left, poking Worf (previous page).]*

PEN PALS
Week of May 1, 1989, No. 141
STARDATE: 42695.3
A little girl (Nikki Cox) contacts Data when her planet is imperiled by a series of violent earthquakes and volcanic eruptions, and Wesley is put in charge of finding the cause of the disturbances and saving the population. **Davies:** Nicholas Cascone. **Sarjenka:** Nikki Cox. **Hildebrandt:** Anne H. Gillespie. **O'Brien:** Colm Meaney. **Alans:** Whitney Rydbeck.

Q WHO?
Week of May 8, 1989, No. 142
STARDATE: 42761.3
Picard's arch-nemesis Q (John de Lancie) tosses the Enterprise into a deadly battle with the Borg, whose collective mind overpowers the starship's defenses. **Ensign Sonya Gomez:** Lycia Naff. **O'Brien:** Colm Meaney. **Guinan:** Whoopi Goldberg.

[Q's third appearance leads to the Federation's first encounter with the Borg—a half-humanoid, half-robotic race living as a single collective entity whose sole purpose is to assimilate other cultures for the sake of gaining new technologies. This episode established the Borg as the most powerful and destructive enemy in Federation history and set the tone for future confrontations—many of these among the most exciting STNG episodes filmed. We learn that the Borg were responsible for the near total destruction of Guinan's race a century earlier. And as Guinan, Whoopi Goldberg shines in a heated exchange with Q over her hatred of the Borg—a confrontation

that will come back to haunt the mischievous alien in the third season's "Déjà Q."

SAMARITAN SNARE
Week of May 15, 1989, No. 143
STARDATE: 42779.1
After Picard is taken to Starbase Scylla 515 for a heart operation, the Enterprise answers a call from a vessel crewed by Pakleds, who take Geordi hostage. **Grebnedlog:** Christopher Collins. **Reginod:** Leslie Morris. **Surgeon:** Daniel Benzali. **Ensign Sonya Gomez:** Lycia Naff. **Biomolecular Physiologist:** Tzi Ma.

[In this episode, Picard tells Wesley that as a 21-year-old ensign he lost his heart —which had to be replaced surgically by an artificial one—in a bar fight with a Nausicaan. Picard would later relive the fight in the sixth season's "Tapestry."]

UP THE LONG LADDER
Week of May 22, 1989, No. 144
STARDATE: 42823.2
The Enterprise encounters two threatened cultures: the Bringloidis, descendants of colonists from Earth; and the Mariposans, clones who desperately need genetic material. **Danilo Odell:** Barrie Ingham. **Granger:** Jon De Vries. **Brenna Odell:** Rosalyn Landor. **O'Brien:** Colm Meaney.

[For sheer fun, this episode, in which Riker plays ladies' man, stands a notch above the rest. The Bringloidis—who don't mind a wee drop or two—prove to be almost as much trouble as the Tribbles once were. Best scene: The leader of the chaste Mariposans—who haven't had sex in decades, finding the mere thought of it repugnant—contemplating having to breed with the earthy, fun-loving Bringloidis on a resettlement world.]

MANHUNT
Week of June 19, 1989, No. 145
STARDATE: 42859.2

En route to a Federation conference, the crew picks up two delegates from the planet Antide III, and gets a surprise visit from Troi's mother, who avidly pursues Capt. Picard. **Lwaxana Troi:** Majel Barrett. **Slade Bender:** Robert Costanzo. **Mr. Homn:** Carel Struycken. **Rex:** Rod Arrants. **O'Brien:** Colm Meaney. **Scarface:** Robert O'Reilly. **Madeline:** Rhonda Aldrich. **Antidian Dignitary:** Mick Fleetwood. **Transport Pilot:** Wren T. Brown.

[Comedy is the name of the game in this episode as Lwaxana—in her second appearance—goes on the prowl for Picard while the captain tries to flee her advances by taking up the holodeck persona of detective Dixon Hill—also for the second time. Luckily for Picard, Lwaxana—in the throes of a female Betazoid midlife cycle that quadruples her sex drive—falls for the bartender instead. A heavily made-up Mick Fleetwood of Fleetwood Mac has a cameo as an Antidian dignitary.]

THE EMISSARY
Week of June 26, 1989, No. 146
STARDATE: 42901.3
A half-Klingon woman (Suzie Plakson) from Worf's past boards the Enterprise as a special agent to intercept a Klingon vessel carrying a crew in cryogenic suspension. **K'Temoc:** Lance Le Gault. **Admiral Gromek:** Georgann Johnson. **O'Brien:** Colm Meaney. **Ensign Clancy:** Anne Ramsay. **Tactical Crewman:** Dietrich Bader.

[Second appearance of actress Suzie Plakson (Love & War), this time as Worf's former lover and future mate, K'Ehleyr—a half-human, half-Klingon diplomat for the Klingon Empire. After their "union" on the holodeck, K'Ehleyr will return—with son Alexander—in the fourth season's "Reunion" to change Worf's life.]

PEAK PERFORMANCE
Week of July 10, 1989, No. 147
STARDATE: 42923.4
Cmdr. Riker and Capt. Picard are pitted against each other in a Starfleet war game, with Picard helming the Enterprise and Riker the Hathaway, an 80-year-old clunker. **Sirna Kollrami:** Roy Brocksmith. **Bractor:** Armin Shimerman. **Ferengi Tactician:** David L. Lander. **Ensign Nagel:** Leslie Neale. **Lieut. Burke:** Glenn Morshower.

[Armin Shimerman's second appearance as a Ferengi—though not the same one.]

SHADES OF GRAY
Week of July 17, 1989, No. 148
STARDATE: 42976.1
Riker (Jonathan Frakes) contracts a mysterious disease that attacks the central nervous system, and Dr. Pulaski tries to save him with a potentially lethal course of treatment. **O'Brien:** Colm Meaney.

[The second-season finale uses Riker's coma-induced dream state as a plot device to replay virtually every significant Riker clip from earlier episodes. These include: "Encounter at Farpoint," "The Naked Now," "The Last Outpost," "Justice," "Angel One," "11001001," "Heart of Glory," "Symbiosis," "Skin of Evil," "Conspiracy," "The Child," "Loud as a Whisper," "Unnatural Selection," "A Matter of Honor," "The Dauphin," "The Icarus Factor" and "Up the Long Ladder."]

ENCOUNTERS

PLANETS: Antide III, Daled IV, Drema IV, Iconia, Klavdia III, Omega IV, Ramatis III, Solais V, Surata IV,
RACES: Antidians, Benzites, Borg, Bringloidis, Ferengi, Mariposans, Pakleds, Zakdorn
SHIPS: Constantinople, Hathaway, Lantree, Pagh, Victory, Yamato

Third Season

The third season would mark *STNG*'s transition from the shadows of its predecessor into its own, as the writing staff matured under the leadership of Michael Piller and day-to-day operations passed from Gene Roddenberry to current executive producer Rick Berman. This season's stories would emphasize character development, humor and scripts with a social conscience—stories that would serve to gain a legion of new and faithful fans. And, thanks in part to a vigorous letter-writing campaign waged by those fans, the third season was to begin with yet another change in medical officers, as Gates McFadden returned to the role of Dr. Beverly Crusher—who, by happy coincidence, had just returned from a year-long assignment at Starfleet Medical. On the uniform front, newly hired costume designer Robert Blackman replaced the men's one-piece jumpsuit that had so constrained Starfleet's finest with the nifty two-piece uniforms still in use. That, of course, led to what fans dubbed the "Picard manoeuvre"—the small tug Patrick Stewart gives to his uniform top any time it starts riding up on him. A small gesture, to be sure, but one that helped define the captain as much as any script detail ever would.

....

EVOLUTION
Week of Sept. 25, 1989, No. 150
STARDATE: 43125.8
En route to the site of a stellar phenomenon, the main computers of the Enterprise malfunction, and the ship is drawn toward the fiery remains of an exploding star. **Dr. Paul Stubbs:** Ken Jenkins. **Eric:** Scott Grimes. **Annette:** Amy O'Neill. **Guinan:** Whoopi Goldberg. **Nurse:** Mary McCusker. **Crewman No. 1:** Randal Patrick.

[What begins as a science experiment for Wesley almost ends in destroying the once-in-a-lifetime project being conducted by Dr. Stubbs aboard the Enterprise. Again, from Data's point of view, the debate about the nature and rights of a sentient being is renewed: Data realizes that he is not alone as a nonorganic being when the microbiotic Nanites begin to evolve and become sentient. Though they threaten both the ship and the experiment Dr.

Stubbs has dedicated his life to, Data refuses to destroy them—instead offering himself as a conduit to communicate with the rapidly evolving beings. This, of course, saves the ship, the experiment and the Nanites' lives. As background detail, the episode notes Dr. Crusher's return, hints at Guinan's past and explains that Wesley learned about baseball from his father.]

....

THE ENSIGNS OF COMMAND
Week of Oct. 2, 1989, No. 149
STARDATE: 43133.3
The Enterprise races against time when an alien race demands all humans living on their planet be evacuated within four days or the entire population will be annihilated. **Ard'rian McKenzie:** Eileen Seeley. **Noe:** Richard Allen. **Haritath:** Mark L. Taylor. **O'Brien:** Colm Meaney. **Gosheven:** Grainger Hines. **Sheliak:** Mart McChesney.

[Seeking to understand human creativity, Data takes up the violin, his progress with

which will be tracked in subsequent episodes. Also note the name "Onizuka" on Data's shuttlepod: Scenic art supervisor Michael Okuda named it after astronaut Ellison Onizuka, who died in January 1986 in the explosion of the U.S. space shuttle Challenger.]

THE SURVIVORS
Week of Oct. 9, 1989, No. 151
STARDATE: 43152.4
Responding to a distress call from a Federation planet, the Away Team finds that all of the inhabitants have been killed except for an elderly couple. **Kevin Uxbridge:** John Anderson. **Rishon Uxbridge:** Anne Haney.

[Sobering episode that reflects on shame, guilt and punishment as Picard discovers that Kevin—who is actually a Douwd, an immortal superbeing disguised as a human —destroyed an entire race, the Husnock, with a single regrettable thought, born out of rage over the death of his wife.]

WHO WATCHES THE WATCHERS?
Week of Oct. 16, 1989, No. 152
STARDATE: 43173.5
Federation anthropologists who are studying the primitive inhabitants of Mintaka III are injured in an explosion. **Nuria:** Kathryn Leigh Scott. **Liko:** Ray Wise. **Dr. Barron:** James Greene. **Oji:** Pamela Segall. **Fento:** John McLiam. **Hali:** James McIntire. **Mary Warren:** Lois Hall.

[The Prime Directive gets another airing when Dr. Crusher beams up the native Liko (played by Ray Wise, later of Twin Peaks*) to save his life.]*

THE BONDING
Week of Oct. 23, 1989, No. 153
STARDATE: 43198.7
During an Away Team survey of a deserted planet, an archeologist (Susan Powell) is killed in an explosion, and the crew tries to comfort her 12-year-old son. **Jeremy Aster:** Gabriel Damon. **Marla**

Aster: Susan Powell. **O'Brien:** Colm Meaney. **Teacher:** Raymond D. Turner.

[In a compelling episode dealing with the loss of a parent, young Jeremy (Gabriel Damon, above) finds comfort in the memories of Worf and Wesley, who both lost parents in childhood—Worf at 6, when his parents were killed during the Khitomer Massacre by the Romulans; and Wesley at 5, when his father Jack was killed during an Away Team mission commanded by Picard. **Best scene:** *Worf leads Jeremy through the Klingon R'uustai bonding ceremony, making him a brother.]*

BOOBY TRAP
Week of Oct. 30, 1989, No. 154
STARDATE: 43205.6
While the Away Team investigates an ancient warship, the Enterprise is bombarded by deadly waves of radiation and crippled by a sudden power loss. **Dr. Leah Brahms:** Susan Gibney. **O'Brien:** Colm Meaney. **Guinan:** Whoopi Goldberg. **Galek Dar:** Albert Hall. **Christy Henshaw:** Julie Warner.

[Picard at his most human, revealing his enthusiastic interest in ancient cultures and technology—a theme often reprised in subsequent episodes. To help spring the

Enterprise from the radiation trap, Geordi calls up the holographic projection of Dr. Leah Brahms, an original designer of the Galaxy-class starship, who becomes Geordi's dream girl. Watch for Julie Warner ("Doc Hollywood") as crew member Christy Henshaw. **Best line:** "You have used the asteroid belt's gravitational pull as a slingshot. Excellent!" marvels Data as Picard takes the helm to personally steer the ship free of the trap.]

THE ENEMY
Week of Nov. 6, 1989, No. 155
STARDATE: 43349.2
Geordi is stranded on a Federation planet where a Romulan ship has crashed, while Dr. Crusher (Gates McFadden) tries to save an injured officer from the downed craft. **Centurion Bochra:** John Snyder. **Cmdr. Tomalak:** Andreas Katsulas. **O'Brien:** Colm Meaney. **Patahk:** Steve Rankin.

[LeVar Burton finally gets an episode in which to shine when Geordi must convince the injured Romulan to combine forces with him to save both their lives. We learn more of the deep-seated hatred between the Klingons and the Romulans, when Worf—orphaned at Khitomer in the Romulan raid—refuses to give blood to save an injured Romulan's life. Showing profound respect for Worf's culture and feelings, Picard, in turn, refuses to order Worf to save his enemy. Picard's respect for Worf's integrity and Klingon heritage will come into play in later episodes when Worf's family honor is questioned.]

THE PRICE
Week of Nov. 13, 1989, No. 156
STARDATE: 43385.6
The Enterprise hosts a delegation that's negotiating for the rights to a wormhole, a shortcut across the galaxy. Meanwhile, Troi becomes romantically involved with one of the delegates. **Devinoni Ral:** Matt McCoy. **Premier Bhavani:** Elizabeth Hoffman. **Dr. Mendoza:** Castulo Guerra.

DaiMon Goss: Scott Thomson. **Dr. Arridor:** Dan Shor. **Leyor:** Kevin Peter Hall. **O'Brien:** Colm Meaney.

[In an episode that raises an ethical debate between Troi and Devinoni over the use of Betazoid powers on humans, comical subplots abound: Riker gets his first chance to act the diplomat when the Ferengi make the Federation delegate too ill to work; and Troi reveals her passion for chocolate. **Best scene:** The look on the Ferengi's faces as the Enterprise crew disappears back through the closing wormhole. The notion of a wormhole would later return as a central feature on Deep Space Nine.]

THE VENGEANCE FACTOR
Week of Nov. 20, 1989, 157
STARDATE: 43421.9
The crew tries to mediate a reconciliation between the Acamarians and the Gatherers, a renegade group that split from the Acamarians a century before. **Yuta:** Lisa Wilcox. **Brull:** Joey Aresco. **Marouk:** Nancy Parsons. **Chorgan:** Stephen Lee. **Volnoth:** Marc Lawrence. **Temarek:** Elkanah Burns.

[Powerful scene in which Riker must overcome his feelings for the beautiful Yuta—in reality a deadly assassin—and kill her before she can start another bloody civil war. As a background note, we learn that Data is stronger than Worf. And watch for the nonspeaking blond Gatherer—he's played by Michael Lamper, Marina Sirtis' real-life husband.]

THE DEFECTOR
Week of Jan. 1, 1990, No. 158
STARDATE: 43462.5
A Romulan defector (James Sloyan) seeking refuge on the Enterprise warns Picard that a major offensive to regain the Neutral Zone will be launched in 48 hours. **Sub.-Lt. Setal/Alidar Jarok:** James Sloyan. **Cmdr. Tomalak:** Andreas Katsulas. **Admiral Haden:** John Hancock. **John Bates:** S.A. Templeman.

[Insight into internal Romulan treachery is provided by the defection of Admiral Jarok. Riker makes reference to the USS Hood, his previous assignment. And watch for Patrick Stewart heavily made up as holodeck character Michael Williams.]

THE HUNTED

Week of Jan. 8, 1990, No. 159
STARDATE: 43489.2

On the planet Angosia III, the crew aids in the capture of a prison escapee (Jeff McCarthy), whose reputation for violence is belied when Troi interviews him. **Roga Danar:** Jeff McCarthy. **Nayrok:** James Cromwell. **O'Brien:** Colm Meaney. **Zaynar:** J. Michael Flynn. **Wagnor:** Andrew Bicknell.

*[Explosive episode dealing with government-sponsored experiments in mind control and biochemical alterations by a planet seeking to join the Federation. High-action chase scenes through little-seen sections of the Enterprise are cleverly juxtaposed with an ongoing debate over the ethics of the experiments and the subsequent incarceration of their subjects. **Best lines:** "A matter for internal security. The age-old cry of the oppressor," muses Picard when the Angosian prime minister warns him not to interfere. And as the prisoner leads him on yet another chase, Worf says, "Danar, you are cunning. You must have Klingon blood."]*

THE HIGH GROUND

Week of Jan. 29, 1990, No. 160
STARDATE: 43510.7

Dr. Crusher is kidnapped by a group of terrorists, and the leader of the Rutian police (Kerrie Keane) is determined not to negotiate for her release. **Kyril Finn:** Richard Cox. **Waiter (Katik Shaw):** Marc Buckland. **Policeman:** Fred G. Smith. **Boy (Ansata):** Christopher Pettiet.

[In an action-packed episode, Picard finally gets to use his fists on the face of an invading terrorist. After Picard is also kidnapped,

the Picard-Crusher relationship is further explored. Watch for Canadian actress Kerrie Keane in the role of Alexana.]

DÉJÀ Q

Week of Feb. 5, 1990, No. 161
STARDATE: 43539.1

Q (John de Lancie), once all-powerful mischief-maker of the universe, is condemned to life as a mortal and seeks sanctuary aboard the Enterprise. **Guinan:** Whoopi Goldberg. **Dr. Garin:** Richard Cansino. **Bre'el Scientist:** Betty Muramoto. **Q2:** Corbin Bernsen.

*[Light-hearted, comical episode in which Q, in his fourth appearance, finally gets what's coming to him—he loses his powers and must depend for his very survival on those he always considered his playthings. Look for L.A. Law's Corbin Bernsen (below)—another longtime Trek fan—as Q2. **Best scenes:** Q orders 10 chocolate sundaes to calm his terrifying new-found hunger; Guinan nearly stabs Q with a fork; Q rewards his new Enterprise friends with a band, cigars, even women, while saving the best reward for Data—an honest-to-good-*

ness human belly laugh. **Best line:** *"Oh, you're so stolid,"* says Q to Riker, who has rejected Q's offer of female companionship. *"You weren't like that before the beard."]*

A MATTER OF PERSPECTIVE
Week of Feb. 12, 1990, No. 162
STARDATE: 43610.4
Riker is accused of murdering a research scientist (Mark Margolis), and the Enterprise holodeck is programmed to re-create the events according to each witness's testimony. **Krag:** Craig Richard Nelson. **Manua Apgar:** Gina Hecht. **O'Brien:** Colm Meaney. **Tayna**: Juli Donald.

[Riker is not the first Starfleet officer to be accused of murder. That dubious honor belonged to the classic Trek's Scotty ("Wolf in the Fold"). This, however, is the first time the holodeck is used to reconstruct the crime.]

YESTERDAY'S ENTERPRISE
Week of Feb. 19, 1990, No. 163
STARDATE: 43625.2
A time rift alters the Enterprise's history and reunites its crew with Tasha Yar (Denise Crosby) and with a ship thought to have been destroyed more than 20 years ago. **Capt. Rachel Garrett:** Tricia O'Neil. **Lieut. (Junior Grade) Richard Castillo:** Christopher McDonald.

[One of STNG's best episodes, with a clever plot twist that has the late Tasha Yar (Denise Crosby, above) coming back to life by means of an alternate time line. A fascinating look at what might have been: In the alternate universe, there has been no Klingon-Federation détente and the ensuing war continues. Note the absence of Worf and Counselor Troi— not to mention the warlike ambience of the alternate Enterprise-D. And in a shocking scene, Riker dies in the alternate time line. Once again, Guinan proves her

wisdom—and her influence with Picard— when she convinces him to send the Enterprise-C back through the time rift to put things right. And in a final gesture, Picard allows Tasha to return with the Enterprise-C, thus saving her from the death she faced in "Skin of Evil." Not the last we'll hear of Tasha Yar.]

THE OFFSPRING
Week of March 12, 1990, No. 164
STARDATE: 43657.0
In an unauthorized experiment, Data builds another android, which chooses to take the form of a human female (Hallie Todd). **Admiral Haftel:** Nicolas Coster. **Lieut. Ballard:** Judyann Elder. **Lal as Robot:** Leonard John Crowfoot.

[First episode directed by Jonathan Frakes, a tear-jerker on the life and death of Lal, Data's daughter. Data demonstrates fatherly traits: stubbornness when he refuses to let Lal leave the Enterprise to live at Starfleet Research; and protectiveness, when—in a lighter moment—he confronts the inquisitive Riker over the first officer's intentions regarding his daughter. Her death, however, gives Data his most poignant human experience to date.]

SINS OF THE FATHER
Week of March 19, 1990, No. 165
STARDATE: 43685.2
Worf meets the brother (Tony Todd) he didn't know he had, and together they go before the Klingon High Council to defend their late father's honor against treason charges. **K'mpec:** Charles Cooper. **Kurn:** Tony Todd. **Duras:** Patrick Massett. **Kahlest:** Thelma Lee.

*[In an episode that allows Michael Dorn to shine, Worf finally meets the brother he never knew. The best Klingon episode to date, providing an excellent depiction of the Klingon homeworld, its culture and ceremonies. Worf shows great respect for his captain when he asks Picard to return to Qo'noS with him, and even greater courage when he allows the lie about his father's treason to stand—thereby averting a Klingon civil war, even though, in so doing, Worf is publicly branded an outcast and a coward. The stage is thus set for the fourth-season cliffhanger, in which Worf sets out to redeem his family's honor. The Klingon phrases in this episode and hereafter were created by linguist Marc Okrand, who developed "The Klingon Dictionary" (see page 52). **Best line:** In response to Worf's request that they return with him to Qo'noS, Picard and Kurn reply, "Jllajnes. ghlj qet jaghmeyjaj." ("I accept with honor. May your enemies run with fear.")]*

ALLEGIANCE
Week of March 26, 1990, No. 166
STARDATE: 43714.1
Picard is kidnapped by an alien force and replaced aboard the Enterprise by a look-alike. **Kova Tholl:** Stephen Markle. **Esoqq:** Reiner Schoener. **Cadet Mitena Haro:** Joycelyn O'Brien. **Alien No. 1:** Jerry Rector. **Alien No. 2:** Jeff Rector.

[Picard is kidnapped for the second time. Patrick Stewart has a little fun in this episode when, as the impostor, he courts a
puzzled Dr. Crusher and leads the Ten Forward crowd in a rousing drinking song.]

CAPTAIN'S HOLIDAY
Week of April 2, 1990, No. 167
STARDATE: 43745.2
Picard's well-deserved vacation is interrupted by Vorgon security agents (Karen Landry, Michael Champion) from the 27th century who are searching for a secret weapon hidden by its time-traveling inventor. **Vash:** Jennifer Hetrick. **Ajur:** Karen Landry. **Boratus:** Michael Champion. **Sovak:** Michael Grodenchik. **Joval:** Deirdre Imershein.

[On the fantasy planet Risa, the captain's much-needed R&R is anything but, in this episode that introduces the infamous Vash—the thief/seductress/con artist who steals the captain's heart while running for her life. The first episode to show Picard in a more relaxed setting with a mood to match. Watch for the bare-chested Stewart in several scenes. Jennifer Hetrick (above, Civil Wars, L.A. Law) appears as Vash.]

TIN MAN
Week of April 23, 1990, No. 168
STARDATE: 43779.3
The Enterprise crew is assigned to carry

a Betazoid Federation emissary (Harry Groener), who's en route to contact a newly discovered life form called Tin Man. **Capt. Robert DeSoto:** Michael Cavanaugh. **Romulan Commander:** Peter Vogt. **O'Brien:** Colm Meaney.

[Watch for Dear John's Harry Groener as the Betazoid Tam Elbrun.]

HOLLOW PURSUITS
Week of April 30, 1990, No. 169
STARDATE: 43807.4
A disturbed crew member (Dwight Schultz) acts out his frustrations in the holodeck and endangers the Enterprise by neglecting his engineering duties. **Lieut. Duffy:** Charley Lang. **O'Brien:** Colm Meaney.

[Dwight Schultz (The A Team) guest stars as Lieut. Barclay, aptly nicknamed Lieut. Broccoli, who has the habit of ducking on to the holodeck whenever life gets too stressful. There, he indulges in his favorite fantasy: dating Troi and dueling with Picard. Some of the best comedic efforts to date: the holodeck version of Troi in flowing robes and bewitching temperament, and a Three Musketeers-style gaggle of officers, including Picard, Data, Geordi and Riker. We also learn that the Enterprise has 4000 power systems. But Geordi's question—and perhaps the most puzzling mystery in Starfleet history—remains unanswered: How did Broccoli ever get through Starfleet Academy?]

THE MOST TOYS
Week of May 7, 1990, No. 170
STARDATE: 43872.2
Data's shuttlecraft explodes, but the crew is forced to proceed on its mission to aid a colony with a contaminated water supply. **Kivas Fajo:** Saul Rubinek. **Palor Toff:** Nehemiah Persoff. **Varria:** Jane Daly. **O'Brien:** Colm Meaney.

[For the second time, Worf is asked to replace a crew member who has "died."

Watch for Canadian actor Saul Rubinek ("The Unforgiven") as Kivas Fajo—a notorious successor to the classic Trek's Harry Mudd—who kidnaps Data to add him to his collection of rare and precious artifacts.]

SAREK
Week of May 14, 1990, No. 171
STARDATE: 43917.4
Sarek (Mark Lenard, below), the venerable Vulcan ambassador, is uncharacteristically moody when aboard the Enterprise for a mission to establish ties with the Legaran. **Perrin:** Joanna Miles. **Ki Mendrossen:** William Denis. **Sakkath:** Rocco Sisto. **O'Brien:** Colm Meaney. **Science Crewman:** John H. Francis.

[The second episode to feature a character from the classic series—this time, Sarek, Spock's Vulcan father. In a long overdue Vulcan storyline, the aging Sarek—who has contracted the Alzheimer-like Bendii syndrome—struggles to contain his emotions. Patrick Stewart has some fine moments as Picard confronts Sarek over his loss of control and deals with the overpowering emotions Sarek temporarily bestows on him via the Vulcan Mind Meld. Picard's bond with Sarek will resurface in the fifth season's two-part "Unification."]

MÉNAGE À TROI
Week of May 28, 1990, No. 172
STARDATE: 43930.7
The Ferengi abduct Counselor Troi and her mother, Lwaxana (Marina Sirtis, Majel Barrett) to study Lwaxana's telepathic powers. **DaiMon Tog:** Frank Corsentino. **Dr. Farek:** Ethan Phillips. **Nibor:** Peter Slutsker. **Reittan Grax:** Rudolph Willrich. **Mr. Homn:** Carel Struycken.

*[Third appearance of the inimitable Lwaxana Troi. Riker and Deanna also get to indulge in an all-too-rare romantic shore leave. And Wesley gets a field promotion to full ensign. **Best scene:** Picard having to feign jealousy over Lwaxana—and spout his beloved Shakespeare—to gain her release.*

TRANSFIGURATIONS
Week of June 4, 1990, No. 173
STARDATE: 43957.2
The Enterprise rescues a humanoid amnesiac (Mark La Mura) who exhibits remarkable healing powers. **John Doe:** Mark La Mura. **Cmdr. Sunad:** Charles Dennis. **Christi Henshaw:** Julie Warner. **O'Brien:** Colm Meaney. **Nurse Temple:** Patti Tippo.

[Worf is killed in a fall but is brought back to life by the mysterious alien.]

THE BEST OF BOTH WORLDS I
Week of June 18, 1990, No. 174
STARDATE: 43989.1
Starfleet Command assigns an ambitious young officer (Elizabeth Dennehy) to help the Enterprise investigate the disappearance of a Federation colony. Part 1 of two. **Admiral J.P. Hanson:** George Murdock. **Guinan:** Whoopi Goldberg. **O'Brien:** Colm Meaney.

[In its most spine-chilling cliffhanger ever, the third season closes on a return appearance by the dreaded Borg—who, having kidnapped Picard, now set about transforming him into the machine-like Locutus

of Borg (above). Every adrenaline-drenched moment is filled with suspense: Will Picard die? Will the Borg destroy the Federation? This episode—STNG's first and most popular cliffhanger—captured the hearts and minds of Trekkers and proved once and for all that STNG had finally come into its own. In a secondary plot line, Riker is pitted against the ambitious Lt.-Cmdr. Shelby (Elizabeth Dennehy, actor Brian Dennehy's daughter), who accuses Riker of laziness when, for the third time, he turns down the command of a ship, the USS Melbourne.]

ENCOUNTERS

PLANETS: Acamar III, Angosia III, Barzan, Bre'el IV, Chalna, Delta Rana IV, Galorndon Core, Lunar V, Mintaka III, Nelvana III, Qo'noS, Risa, Rutia IV, Tanuga IV, Tau Cygna V
RACES: Acamarians, Angosians, Barzans, Borg, Chalnoth, Chrysalians, Douwd, Gatherers, Husnock, Klingons, Menthars, Mintakans, Mizarians, Promellians, Romulans, Rutians, Sheliak, Tanugans, Vorgons, Vulcans, Zalkonians
SHIP: Enterprise NCC-1701-C

Fourth Season

The fourth season couldn't come fast enough for the millions of Trekkers who impatiently awaited the resolution of the nail-biting Borg cliffhanger. Could Picard be rescued from the Borg? Could the Borg be stopped from destroying the Federation? The pent-up suspense held over the summer and helped make "The Best of Both Worlds II" an unqualified success. That fanfare had barely died down when "Legacy," *STNG*'s record-setting 80th episode, aired in late October, thereby breaking the mark set by the original's 79-episode run. The fourth season would also mark the return of many previous guests—including Q, Lwaxana Troi, Lieut. Barclay, Dr. Leah Brahms and the Traveler—back to pursue further adventures aboard the Enterprise. And, in what was to become the season's dominant theme, nine of the first 11 episodes dealt with family: Worf introduces his foster parents, meets his son and avenges his wife's death; Picard returns home to reconcile with the brother he hasn't seen in 20 years; Data meets his father, battles his evil twin and learns about love. This was also the season of maturity: Wesley takes his leave of the Enterprise to study at Starfleet Academy; O'Brien gets married; and Worf takes responsiblity for his son and his life as a Klingon. Altogether, the fourth season featured the greatest number of episodes ever to deal with character development and would become, in the opinion of many fans—as in ours—its best season.

THE BEST OF BOTH WORLDS II
Week of Sept. 24, 1990, No. 175
STARDATE: 44001.4
Conclusion. The Borg have turned Picard into a half-Borg, half-human creature, and are using him in their plot to conquer Earth.
Lt.-Cmdr. Shelby: Elizabeth Dennehy.
Admiral Hanson: George Murdock.
O'Brien: Colm Meaney. **Guinan:** Whoopi Goldberg. **Ensign Gleason:** Todd Merrill.

[In a conclusion as suspenseful and well written as the previous season's cliffhanger, the action is neatly interwoven with the all-too-human dilemmas faced by members of the crew—including Riker, who must take command of the ship while contending with his overly ambitious first officer, and Guinan, who can't bear to witness the Borg destroying humanity like they destroyed her people—but still manages to give Riker some excellent advice. Shedding a single tear to signal Picard's presence, Patrick Stewart gives a commanding performance as Locutus of Borg—a creation of the Borg's cybernetic implants and his own hot-wired DNA—who leads the Borg in a devastating attack against Starfleet's armada, destroying 39 ships, including the USS Melbourne, at a cost of more than 11,000 lives. But it's Data who saves the day by sending the Borg into regeneration mode when he correctly interprets Picard's single utterance ("Sleep"). While it will take the Federation a year to rebuild the fleet, the consequences of that tragedy would return in the pilot episode of Deep Space Nine, when Picard would face the animosity of Cmdr. Benjamin Sisko, whose wife was killed during the attack.]

FAMILY
Week of Oct. 1, 1990, No. 178
STARDATE: 44012.3
Picard has a strained reunion with his older brother (Jeremy Kemp) when he returns to his home town; while Worf's adoptive parents (Theodore Bikel and Georgia Brown) are hurt by his distant manner. **Robert Picard:** Jeremy Kemp. **Marie Picard:** Samantha Eggar. **Sergey Rozhenko:** Theodore Bikel. **Helena Rozhenko:** Georgia Brown. **Louis:** Dennis Creaghan. **O'Brien:** Colm Meaney. **Guinan:** Whoopi Goldberg. **Jack R. Crusher:** Doug Wert. **Rene Picard:** David Tristan Birkin.

[A star-studded guest cast enlivens this revealing episode about families—those of Picard, Worf and the Crushers. Jeremy Kemp (above) is outstanding as the older brother Picard fell out with 20 years earlier, and who goads Jean-Luc once more into a memorable mud tussle, while helping him face his guilt over the Borg disaster. In a more comedic vein, Theodore Bikel and Georgia Brown shine as Worf's adoptive parents, who, while supportive of their son over his recent Klingon discommendation, can still make Worf blush with embarrassment as only a parent can. And in the most touching storyline, Wesley learns something of his late father, Jack, when Beverly finally lets him see the haunting holotape Jack made just after Wesley was born. Watch for the wine Robert gives Jean-Luc to be shared in the subsequent fourth-season episode "First Contact." Also, the full name of Colm Meaney's character, Miles Edward O'Brien, is at last revealed.]

BROTHERS
Week of Oct. 8, 1990, No. 177
STARDATE: 44085.7

Data begins to malfunction and takes control of the Enterprise, while a young passenger is dangerously ill and in need of a treatment at a nearby Starbase. **Jake Potts:** Cory Danziger. **O'Brien:** Colm Meaney. **Willie (Potts):** Adam Ryen. **Ensign Kopf:** James Lashly. **Lore/Dr. Noonian Soong:** Brent Spiner.

[In an episode written by executive producer Rick Berman, Brent Spiner outdoes himself in a triple role as Data; as Data's creator, Dr. Noonian Soong; and as Data's evil twin, Lore, first encountered in the first season's "Datalore." Called home by his creator—long since presumed dead—Data meets the reclusive genius, who has at last perfected a chip that will allow Data to feel the human emotions for which he has longed. That opportunity vanishes when Lore—who turns up in response to the same signal—tricks Soong, stealing the chip and leaving the inventor fatally injured. **Best scene:** In saying goodbye to the man he has only just met, Data calls Soong Father and is left to ponder what he might have known. While Data would be reunited with his father in the sixth season's "Birthright I," he would not again face the evil Lore until the seventh season's "Descent II."

SUDDENLY HUMAN
Week of Oct. 15, 1990, No. 176
STARDATE: 44143.7
The Away Team finds that a Talarian ship in distress has a crew of teenagers, one of

them a human (Chad Allen) who shows signs of severe abuse. **Capt. Endar:** Sherman Howard. **Admiral Connaught Rossa:** Barbara Townsend.

[Picard's edgy relationship with children is examined when the captain must determine why Jono, the human child raised by aliens, doesn't want to go home to his human family. Chad Allen (Dr. Quinn, Medicine Woman) gives an honest portrayal of Jono, a child torn apart by being forced to choose between the alien father he knows and loves, and the human family seeking his return.]

REMEMBER ME
Week of Oct. 22, 1990, No. 179
STARDATE: 44161.2
People aboard the Enterprise are vanishing at an alarming rate, and no one except Dr. Crusher has any memory of their existence. **Traveler:** Eric Menyuk. **Commander Dalen Quaice, M.D.:** Bill Erwin. **O'Brien:** Colm Meaney.

[Stellar performance by Gates McFadden, who carries the storyline solo for part of the episode. Left to solve the mystery or die in the incredible shrinking universe that—from her perspective—has invaded the Enterprise, Dr. Crusher argues with the computer while her crewmates double-talk and disappear, and begins to doubt her sanity as she is left entirely alone. The recurring Star Trek theme of an alternative universe provides the opportunity here to learn more about Beverly's background, her thoughts and feelings as she works to discover the key to the mystery. Watch for a second appearance by the Traveler, who returns to help Wesley save his mother.]

LEGACY
Week of Oct. 29, 1990, No. 180
STARDATE: 44215.2
On the planet Turkana IV, birthplace of the late Tasha Yar, two warring factions

hinder the Away Team's rescue of a marooned Federation crew. **Ishara Yar:** Beth Toussaint. **Hayne:** Don Mirault. **O'Brien:** Colm Meaney. **Tan Tsu:** Vladimir Velasco. **Coalition Lieut.:** Christopher Michael.

[The milestone 80th STNG episode, besting the 79-episode run of the classic series. Picking up on the Tasha Yar storyline, the crew encounters her long-lost younger sister, Ishara (Beth Toussaint), a member of one of the two warring factions who befriends the crew as a means to penetrate the defenses of her enemies. Both Picard and Data are drawn to Ishara out of friendship for Tasha, but it is Data who gets an unexpected lesson in betrayal when the younger Yar nearly kills him in pursuit of her mission.]

REUNION
Week of Nov. 5, 1990, No. 181
STARDATE: 44246.3
K'mpec (Charles Cooper), the dying Klingon leader, asks Picard to find out which of the two rivals for his position has been poisoning him; and Worf has a reunion with his former mate. **K'Ehleyr:** Suzie Plakson. **Gowron:** Robert O'Reilly. **Duras:** Patrick Massett. **Alexander:** Jon Steuer. **Security Guard:** Michael Rider. **Transporter Chief Hubble:** April Grace. **Guard No. 1:** Basil Wallace. **Klingon:** Mirron E. Willis.

[In Jonathan Frakes' second directorial stint, actress Suzie Plakson (above, Love & War) returns in the role of Klingon Ambassador K'Ehleyr—Worf's half-human former love and the mother of his unknown son, Alexander. The episode is rife with both passion and political intrigue, as Worf rekindles his romance with K'Ehleyr and Picard assists dying Klingon leader K'mpec to perform the ritual selecting a new leader, while attempting to unmask K'Mpec's assassin. Duras—the Klingon who implicated Worf's father in

[Riker discovers, if only temporarily, what it's like to be both captain of the Enterprise and the father of a teenage son. His fantasy love, Minuet, makes a return appearance in a holotape of his dream life, which leads him to discover the truth about his surroundings—seemingly rigged by the Romulan Tomalak. Riker's fantasy future served as a neat device to catch a glimpse of the Federation as it could evolve 16 years hence—including a bearded Admiral Picard and a married Troi. Third appearance by Andreas Katsulas as Tomalak.]

the Khitomer Massacre to hide his own father's guilt and now a contender to succeed K'mpec—kills K'Ehleyr when she rightly suspects him of the crime. Crossing the thin line of his restraint, Worf finally gives in to his Klingon rage and kills Duras for murdering his mate and dishonoring his father. While not yet at liberty to reclaim his family's honor—that would wait until the season's cliffhanger, "Redemption"—Worf cannot publicly acknowledge Alexander as his son and sends him to live with his own foster parents so as to spare the youngster the shame of his discommendation. Later played by Brian Bonsall ("Blank Check," Family Ties), Alexander would return to live with Worf in the fifth season's "New Ground."]

FINAL MISSION
Week of Nov. 19, 1990, No. 183
STARDATE: 44307.3
In honor of Wesley's acceptance into the Starfleet Academy, Picard asks him to come on a mission to Pentarus V, but they're forced to make an emergency landing on a lifeless moon, where Picard is critically injured in a rock slide. **Dirgo:** Nick Tate. **Chairman Songi:** Kim Hamilton. **Ensign Tess Allenby:** Mary Kohnert.

[Wil Wheaton gives his best performance in this episode marking his departure from the regular cast, as Wesley—like Picard years earlier—finally gets accepted at Starfleet Academy, on his second attempt. Touching moments as Wesley comforts an injured Picard, trying to keep him alive long enough to be rescued. Picard, in turn, admits how proud he is of Wesley, and tells him of Boothby, the Academy groundskeeper and Picard's mentor, who would later be seen in the fifth season's "The First Duty." Watch for Nick Tate (Space: 1999) as Dirgo.]

FUTURE IMPERFECT
Week of Nov. 12, 1990, No. 182
STARDATE: 44286.5
After an aborted Away Team mission, Riker awakens in sick bay to an aging Dr. Crusher, who explains that a long-dormant virus has wiped out his memory of the past 16 years. **Ambassador Tomalak:** Andreas Katsulas. **Jean-Luc/Ethan:** Chris Demetral. **Minuet:** Carolyn McCormick. **Nurse Alyssa Ogawa:** Patti Yasutake. **Transporter Chief Hubbell:** April Grace. **Transporter Chief:** George O'Hanlon Jr. **Barash:** Chris Demetral.

THE LOSS
Week of Dec. 31, 1990, No. 184
STARDATE: 44356.9
While the Enterprise is swept into the gravitational wake of two-dimensional life forms, Troi (Marina Sirtis) realizes her powers have left her. **Ensign Janet Brooks:** Kim Braden. **Ensign Tess Allenby:** Mary Kohnert. **Guinan:** Whoopi Goldberg.

[In an episode that focuses on Troi's crisis of confidence over the loss of her empathic powers, Marina Sirtis provides shades of depth and vulnerability to Deanna's in-control self. We also see how strong the Riker-Troi relationship continues to be.]

DATA'S DAY
Week of Jan. 7, 1991, No. 185
STARDATE: 44390.1
Data faces the twin tasks of giving away the bride (Rosalind Chao) at Chief O'Brien's wedding and escorting Vulcan Ambassador T'Pel aboard to negotiate a treaty with the Romulans. **O'Brien:** Colm Meaney. **Ambassador T'Pel (Sub Commander Selok):** Sierra Pecheur. **Admiral Mendak:** Alan Scarfe. **Transporter Chief Hubble:** April Grace. **V'Sal:** Shelly Desai.

[In a highly creative day-in-the-life episode, the action unfolds from the perspective of a very busy Data—the only 24-hour-a-day being on the ship—who must contend with bride Keiko's change of heart on the eve of her wedding to Miles O'Brien as well as Ambassador T'Pel's attempt to extract security information for which she has not been cleared. Following the Ambassador's apparent death in an unexplained transporter accident, Data turns once again to his Sherlock Holmes persona to unravel the mystery—all the while attempting to help Keiko sort out her feelings for O'Brien. Successful on both counts, Data ends his day by walking Keiko down the aisle in a marriage ceremony performed by Picard. First glimpse of Data's cat, possibly Riker's least favorite creature. Best scene: Dr. Crusher teaching Data how to dance for the wedding.]

THE WOUNDED
Week of Jan. 28, 1991, No. 186
STARDATE: 44429.6
The Enterprise intercepts a starship whose renegade captain (Bob Gunton) is attacking the Cardassians, former enemies of the Federation. **Keiko Ishikawa O'Brien:** Rosalind Chao. **Gul Macet:** Marc Alaimo. **Miles O'Brien:** Colm Meaney. **Glinn Telle:** Marco Rodriguez. **Glinn Daro:** Time Winters. **Admiral Haden:** John Hancock.

[First real look at the Federation's newest enemies, the Cardassians, as well as an in-depth look at Miles O'Brien and his relationship with his former captain, Benjamin Maxwell. Colm Meaney does a star turn in this episode, with O'Brien being the only one able to convince Maxwell to stand down in the face of war.]

DEVIL'S DUE
Week of Feb. 4, 1991, No. 187
STARDATE: 44474.5
The Enterprise comes to the aid of the Ventaxians, who are faced with the prospect of fulfilling a diabolical contract made by their ancestors. **Ardra:** Marta DuBois. **Dr. Clarke:** Paul Lambert. **Jared:** Marcello Tubert. **Devil Monster:** Thad Lamey. **Klingon Monster:** Tom Magee. **Marley:** William Glover.

[Watch for Marta DuBois (Magnum's ex on Magnum, P.I.) as the con-artist-cum-devil Ardra, whose sexual advances Picard refuses—in retaliation for which she decides to make the Enterprise disappear.]

CLUES
Week of Feb. 11, 1991, No. 188
STARDATE: 44502.7
Picard (Patrick Stewart) suspects Data (Brent Spiner) of lying about a phenomenon that rendered the crew unconscious. **O'Brien:** Colm Meaney. **Ensign McKnight:** Pamela Winslow. **Madeline:** Rhonda Aldrich. **Guinan:** Whoopi Goldberg. **Nurse Alyssa Ogawa:** Patti Yasutake. **Gunman:** Thomas Knickerbocker.

[Third appearance of Picard's holodeck persona, detective Dixon Hill.]

FIRST CONTACT
Week of Feb. 18, 1991, No. 189

STARDATE: Unknown

While on a first-contact mission to a planet on the verge of space travel, Riker (Jonathan Frakes) is captured and accused of leading an alien invasion. **Chancellor Avel Durken:** George Coe. **Mirasta:** Carolyn Seymour. **Berel:** George Hearn. **Krola:** Michael Ensign. **Nilrem:** Steven Anderson. **Dr. Tava:** Sachi Parker. **Lanel:** Bebe Neuwirth.

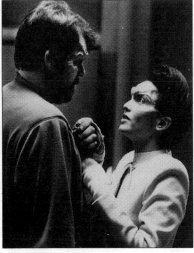

*[Interesting examination of the fear of aliens as told from the planet's point of view instead of the Federation's. This first-contact mission is one of nine occasions on which Picard is later accused by Admiral Satie of having violated the Prime Directive ("The Drumhead"). We also learn that a long-ago and unsuccessful first-contact mission led to years of Federation-Klingon enmity. Watch for Sachi Parker, Shirley MacLaine's daughter, in the role of Dr. Tava. **Best scene:** Bebe Neuwirth (Lilith on Cheers) has a memorable cameo (above) as a nurse whose greatest fantasy is to have sex with an alien—the injured Riker, who seems in no position to refuse.]*

GALAXY'S CHILD
Week of March 11, 1991, No. 190
STARDATE: 44614.6

The Enterprise serves as a surrogate mother to a newborn energy being; Geordi (LeVar Burton) faces the real Dr. Brahms (Susan Gibney), whom he once re-created on the holodeck. **Ensign Rager:** Lanei Chapman. **Ensign Pavlik:** Jana Marie Hupp. **Guinan:** Whoopi Goldberg. **Transporter Chief Hubble:** April Grace.

[Second appearance of Susan Gibney, this time as the real Dr. Leah Brahms— Geordi's fantasy woman and an original designer of the Enterprise—who turns out to be noticeably different from Geordi's holodeck creation, in that she's married and just a tad more critical than in his fantasy ("Booby Trap"). Geordi's struggle to overcome his discomfort around women becomes more apparent in this episode, although he does manage to make friends with Leah—even after she discovers his fantasy program.]

NIGHT TERRORS
Week of March 18, 1991, No. 191
STARDATE: 44631.2

The Enterprise encounters the same fate as the ship it was sent to rescue—drifting in a section of space where dream deprivation can drive the crew to insanity and murder. **Keiko O'Brien:** Rosalind Chao. **Andrus Hagan:** John Vickery. **Ensign Gillespie:** Duke Moosekian. **Ensign Peeples:** Craig Hurley. **Ensign Kenny Lin:** Brian Tochi. **Ensign Rager:** Lanei Chapman. **O'Brien:** Colm Meaney. **Guinan:** Whoopi Goldberg. **Capt. Chantal Zaheva:** Deborah Taylor.

[In an episode that, for once, lets Troi's empathic powers save the ship, watch for Brian Tochi—Leonardo of "The Teenage Mutant Ninja Turtles"—as Ensign Kenny Lin. Years earlier, Tochi appeared as the young Ray Tsingtao on the classic Trek's "And the Children Shall Lead."]

IDENTITY CRISIS
Week of March 25, 1991, No. 192
STARDATE: 44664.5
Five years after investigating a mysteriously abandoned outpost, members of the Away Team begin to exhibit unusual symptoms—and an overwhelming urge to return to the planet. **Lt.-Cmdr. Susanna Leitjen:** Maryann Plunkett. **Nurse Alyssa Ogawa:** Patti Yasutake. **Lieut. Hickman:** Amick Byram. **Transporter Chief Hendrick:** Dennis Madalone. **Ensign Graham:** Mona Grudt. **Brevelle:** Paul Thompkins.

[A strong episode for LeVar Burton, in which La Forge is reunited with a former USS Victory shipmate—who, with Geordi, participated in an Away Team mission to the planet Tarchannen III five years earlier, where an unseen parasite entered—and is now transforming—their bodies.]

NTH DEGREE
Week of April 1, 1991, No. 193
STARDATE: 44704.2
A shy, introspective crewman (Dwight Schultz) is transformed into a superbeing who interfaces with the ship's computer—taking the Enterprise into an uncharted

realm of space. **"Einstein":** Jim Morton. **Cytherian:** Kay E. Kuter. **Lieut. Linda Larson:** Saxon Trainor. **Ensign April Anaya:** Page Leong. **Lieut. Reginald Barclay:** Dwight Schultz. **Ensign Brower:** David Coburn.

[Dwight Schultz (below left) returns as Lieut. Barclay, in an episode that bears a passing resemblance to the classic Trek's *"Where No Man Has Gone Before."]*

QPID
Week of April 22, 1991, No. 194
STARDATE: 44741.9
Picard's old foe Q (John de Lancie) transforms the captain and crew into Robin Hood and his Merry Men—and Picard's old flame Vash (Jennifer Hetrick) into Maid Marian in distress. **Sir Guy:** Clive Revill. **Servant:** Joi Staton.

[A fantasy episode in the tradition of the classic Trek's *"Shore Leave," and one of STNG's most humorous outings. In his fifth appearance, John de Lancie is at his mischievous best as the infuriating Q, and Jennifer Hetrick returns as Picard's love interest, Vash. To repay the favor Picard did him in the previous season's "Déjà Q," the bad boy of the universe simulates the Sherwood Forest fantasy to get Picard and Vash to admit their true feelings for one another. But in a promising twist of fate— to be explored in a later episode of* Deep Space Nine—*Vash declares her intention to travel the galaxy with Q, rather than stay with Picard.* **Best line:** *Forced to join Robin Hood's band of thieves, a protesting Worf declares, "I am NOT a merry man!"]*

THE DRUMHEAD
Week of April 29, 1991, No. 195
STARDATE: 44769.2
An investigation into espionage aboard the Enterprise escalates into a witch hunt when a retired Starfleet admiral (Jean Simmons) suspects treachery and implicates Picard. **Sabin Genestra:** Bruce French. **Simon Tarses:** Spencer Garrett. **Lieut. J'Ddan:**

Henry Woronicz. **Admiral Thomas Henry:** Earl Billings. **Nellen Tore:** Ann Shea.

[In a chilling clip episode—Jonathan Frakes' third as director—Admiral Norah Satie leads a 24th-century witch hunt for conspirators who don't exist. The admiral accuses Picard of violating the Prime Directive nine times ("Justice," "Angel One," "Pen Pals," "Up the Long Ladder," "The Ensigns of Command," "Who Watches the Watchers?" "The High Ground," "Legacy" and "First Contact.") Jean Simmons gives an extremely effective portrayal of a woman whose bitter rage overwhelms her sense of justice.]

··

HALF A LIFE
Week of May 6, 1991, No. 196
STARDATE: 44805.3
Troi's mother, Lwaxana (Majel Barrett), is smitten with a scientist (David Ogden Stiers, right) whose culture demands he return to his home planet to commit ritual suicide. **Dara:** Michelle Forbes. **B'tardat:** Terence McNally. **O'Brien:** Colm Meaney. **Mr. Homn:** Carel Struycken.

[In sad, sweet episode, David Ogden Stiers (M*A*S*H) and Majel Barrett are well paired as lovers forced to separate when he must go home to die. On board to conduct an experiment that may save his world's dying star, the reserved Dr. Timicin is at first bewildered, then enchanted, by the outgoing Lwaxana Troi, back in her fourth visit to the Enterprise. Persuaded by his new-found love to seek asylum rather than abandon his work and life to ritual suicide, the 60-year-old Timicin is confronted by his daughter, Dara (Michelle Forbes, who would return in the fifth season as Ensign Ro), who begs her father to remain true to his heritage and go through with their culture's "resolution." In a tearful exchange that allows Majel Barrett to display her dramatic talents, Timicin tells Lwaxana of his decision to meet his proscribed destiny. In the episode's touching

final scene, Lwaxana—as one of Timicin's loved ones—decides to accompany him to the planet to be with the scientist in his final moments.]

··

THE HOST
Week of May 13, 1991, No. 197
STARDATE: 44821.3
Dr. Crusher's love affair with an alien ambassador (Franc Luz) becomes complicated when the ambassador turns out to be a small parasitic creature that inhabits host bodies. **Governor Leka Trion:** Barbara Tarbuck. **Kareel:** Nicole Orth-Pallavicini. **Kalin Trose:** William Newman. **Nurse Ogawa:** Patti Yasutake. **Lathal Bine:** Robert Harper.

[Beverly (Gates McFadden) finally gets to display her passionate side when she falls in love with Odan, a Trillian diplomat, and is torn when she discovers the true nature of his symbiotic relationship with his host body. The Trill species would later return on Deep Space Nine *in the character of Jadzia Dax.* **Best scene:** *Odan, after being temporarily housed in Riker's body when his first body dies, convinces Beverly to continue their affair, and they spend one more night together.]*

THE MIND'S EYE
Week of May 27, 1991, No. 198
STARDATE: 44885.5
The Romulans capture and brainwash Geordi (LeVar Burton), using him in their plan to foment rebellion at a Klingon outpost. **Ambassador Kell:** Larry Dobkin. **Taibak:** John Fleck. **Governor Vagh:** Edward Wiley. **O'Brien:** Colm Meaney. **Computer Voice:** Majel Barrett.

IN THEORY
Week of June 3, 1991, No. 199
STARDATE: 44932.3
While Picard (Patrick Stewart) navigates the Enterprise through an unstable region of space, Data (Brent Spiner) tries to fathom the amorous advances of a crewmate (Michele Scarabelli). **Keiko O'Brien:** Rosalind Chao. **O'Brien:** Colm Meaney. **Ensign McKnight:** Pamela Winslow. **Guinan:** Whoopi Goldberg.

[In a seriocomic episode that marks Patrick Stewart's debut in the director's seat, Data comes close to learning—firsthand—the meaning of love. Despite his well-meaning attempt to create a program to provide himself with a guide to love, Data doesn't quite get it, and when Ensign Jenna D'Sora realizes that she can't fall in love with a machine, Data's left holding the program and his cat, Spot, while D'Sora walks sadly out the door.]

REDEMPTION I
Week of June 17, 1991, No. 200
STARDATE: 44995.3
A power struggle within the High Council threatens the Klingon Empire, forcing Worf (Michael Dorn) to choose between continuing his service on the Enterprise or returning to his people. **Gowron:** Robert O'Reilly. **Cmdr. Kurn:** Tony Todd. **Lursa:** Barbara March. **B'Etor:** Gwynyth Walsh. **K'Tal:** Ben Slack. **General Movar:** Nicholas Kepros. **Toral:** J.D. Cullum. **Guinan:** Whoopi Goldberg. **Klingon First Officer:** Tom Ormeny. **Computer Voice:** Majel Barrett. **Cmdr. Sela:** Denise Crosby. **Helmsman:** Clifton Jones.

[The series' second cliffhanger pits Worf against traitors on his homeworld, in the final chapter of the saga that began in the earlier "Sins of the Father" and "Reunion" episodes. Michael Dorn has some of his best moments as Worf reclaims his father's honor and resigns his Starfleet commission to fight for Gowron in the Klingon civil war. And in STNG's most surprising plot twist, Denise Crosby (above) returns as Romulan Cmdr. Sela, Tasha Yar's daughter by her forced marriage to her Romulan abductor— an explanation that would have to wait until the fifth season's return. Watch for Canadian actresses Barbara March and Gwynyth Walsh as the sisters of Duras.]

ENCOUNTERS

PLANETS: Alfa 117, Earth, Kaelon II, Pentarus V, Tarchannen III, Turkana IV, Ventax II
RACES: Cardassians, Cytherians, Klingons, Malcorians, Paxans, Romulans, Talarians, Ventaxians
SHIPS: Brattain, Kyushu, Melbourne, Phoenix, Tolstoy

Fifth Season

The fifth season began on a high note, with celebrations to mark *Star Trek*'s 25th anniversary—not bad for a show NBC tried to kill more than once. By that fall, *STNG* was achieving weekly ratings that—had it been seen on a U.S. network—would have placed it on the Nielsen Top 10 prime-time list every week without fail. And while top-notch scripts and consistently fine performances should have placed the series within serious Emmy contention, its lack of a network berth helped relegate the show to a mere handful of technical awards. Stories this season would focus on character development, social commentary, and overcoming personal differences to fight for a common goal. Issues such as vengeance, sexual preference, euthanasia and genetic engineering were explored without preaching and without forsaking the action-adventure mode that was *Star Trek*'s hallmark. But, alas, it was to be a season without Q—the roguish mischief-maker and fan favorite. And, sadly, October brought the death of series creator Gene Roddenberry, who died knowing that the vision he began would continue to live long and prosper.

REDEMPTION II
Week of Sept. 23, 1991, No. 201
STARDATE: 45020.4
Picard (Patrick Stewart) initiates a Federation blockade against the Romulans in hopes of exposing their alliance with the Duras family in the Klingon civil war. **Cmdr. Sela:** Denise Crosby. **Cmdr. Kurn:** Tony Todd. **Lursa:** Barbara March. **B'Etor:** Gwynyth Walsh. **Toral:** J.D. Cullum. **Gowron:** Robert O'Reilly. **Capt. Larg:** Michael G. Hagerty. **Admiral Shanthi:** Fran Bennett. **Gen. Movar:** Nicholas Kepros. **O'Brien:** Colm Meaney. **Lt.-Cmdr. Christopher Hobson:** Timothy Carhart. **Guinan:** Whoopi Goldberg. **Kulge:** Jordan Lund. **Ensign Craig:** Clifton Jones.

[A second action-packed conclusion to a season cliffhanger—with one of the most entertaining plot twists ever developed for a science fiction series: Seemingly back from the dead, Denise Crosby pops up in the role of Tasha Yar's half-Romulan daughter, Sela, who plots with the sisters of Duras to initiate civil war in the Klingon Empire and destroy the Federation. Another fine performance by Michael Dorn, who plays both sides of Worf's loyalties—to his Klingon homeworld and to the Federation—with equal conviction. And Data finally commands a ship in this episode, handling the crew's resistance to his orders admirably well. **Best scene:** In explaining her uncanny resemblance to Tasha Yar, Sela reveals her lingering guilt over betraying her mother for trying to escape the Romulans.]

DARMOK
Week of Sept. 30, 1991, No. 202
STARDATE: 45047.2
While initiating relations with the Tamarians—whose language is incomprehensible to humans—Picard and the captain of the Tamarian ship (Paul Winfield) are transported to a planet where both face a fierce beast. **Tamarian First Officer:** Richard Allen. **O'Brien:** Colm Meaney.

[With the two captains cooperating (rather than fighting one another as in the classic Trek's "Arena"), Picard learns a tough lesson on the value of communication when his new-found ally (Paul Winfield, above, with Patrick Stewart) is killed by the beast they fought together—and he must use his limited knowledge of the Tamarian language to praise the dead captain's courage, lest the Tamarian crew open fire on the Enterprise. Watch for Ashley Judd (Sisters) as Ensign Lefler, who would appear later in the season as Wesley's love interest in "The Game."]

ENSIGN RO
Week of Oct. 7, 1991, No. 203
STARDATE: 45076.3
During their investigation of a Bajoran terrorist attack on a Federation colony, Picard (Patrick Stewart) and a strong-willed Bajoran ensign (Michelle Forbes) uncover a conspiracy by a high-ranking Starfleet officer. **Keeve Falor:** Scott Marlowe. **Gul Dolak:** Frank Collison. **Orta:** Jeffrey Hayenga. **Transporter Technician Collins:** Harley Venton. **Barber Mot:** Ken Thorley. **Admiral Kennelly:** Cliff Potts. **Guinan:** Whoopi Goldberg.

[Michelle Forbes—Dr. Timicin's daughter in "Half a Life"—appears as Ro Laren, the strong-willed Bajoran with a troubled past. Ro is the first recurring crew member to display aggression and impatience—creating serious discussion among the officers. Guinan reveals her intuitive side in reading through Ro's tough façade to see the insecure, vulnerable person within. With the appearance of the Bajorans, this episode lays the foundations for much of Deep Space Nine.]

SILICON AVATAR
Week of Oct. 14, 1991, No. 204
STARDATE: 45122.3
The Enterprise comes in contact with a destructive entity that Picard (Patrick Stewart) believes should be communicated with—but a scientist (Ellen Geer) studying it has different plans. **Carmen Davila:** Susan Diol.

[The return of the Crystalline Entity ("Datalore") sets the stage for an engaging clash between Picard—remaining faithful to his mission to seek out new life—and Dr. Kila Marr, the scientist obsessed with avenging her son's death on Omicron Theta—Data's home planet—at the hands of the entity. Although initially hostile to Data—accusing him of luring the entity to Melona IV as Lore had done on Omicron Theta—she bonds with him after realizing that his programming contains the memories of Omicron Theta's inhabitants, including those of her son. Brent Spiner solos on guitar as Data's interest in music progresses.]

DISASTER
Week of Oct. 21, 1991, No. 205
STARDATE: 45156.1
While hosting the winners of a primary school science contest, the Enterprise is completely disabled by a rare natural phenomenon, leaving Troi (Marina Sirtis) in command on the bridge. **Keiko O'Brien:** Rosalind Chao. **Miles O'Brien:** Colm Meaney. **Ensign Ro:** Michelle Forbes.

STAR TREK © 1994 PARAMOUNT PICTURES (2)

Marissa: Erika Flores. **Jay Gordon:** John Christian Graas. **Patterson:** Max Supera. **Ensign Mandel:** Cameron Arnett. **Lieut. Monroe:** Jana Marie Hupp.

[Splendid high-tension episode bringing out the crew's lesser known strengths: The injured Picard must comfort three frightened children; Worf must tend to the wounded and deliver Keiko's baby; and an uncertain Troi must take command, finding the courage to make crucial decisions in the nick of time. Watch for Erika Flores (Dr. Quinn, Medicine Woman) as Marissa. **Best scene:** *A panicky Worf orders Keiko to give birth "immediately."]*

THE GAME
Week of Oct. 28, 1991, No. 206
STARDATE: 45028.2
Riker is given an electronic mind game that proves addictive to everyone on board except a vacationing Wesley (Wil Wheaton), who suspects the game's real purpose. **Ensign Robin Lefler:** Ashley Judd. **Etana Jol:** Katherine Moffat. **O'Brien:** Colm Meaney. **Nurse Alyssa Ogawa:** Patti Yasutake. **Ensign:** Diane M. Hurley.

[Wil Wheaton's first guest appearance since leaving the show in the fourth season. Ashley Judd's second appearance as Ensign Lefler, to whom the vacationing Wesley takes an immediate shine.]

UNIFICATION I
Week of Nov. 4, 1991, No. 208
STARDATE: 45236.4
Disguised as Romulans, Picard and Data travel to Romulus to investigate the unauthorized mission of the Federation's most famous ambassador—Mr. Spock (Leonard Nimoy). **Perrin:** Joanna Miles. **Capt. K'Vada:** Stephen D. Root. **Klim Dokachin:** Graham Jarvis. **Senator Pardek:** Malachi Throne. **Proconsul Neral:** Norman Large. **B'iJik:** Eric Avari. **Admiral Brackett:** Karen Hensel. **Sarek:** Mark Lenard. **Soup Woman:** Mimi Cozzens. **Computer Voice:** Majel Barrett.

[The third and best appearance of a character carried over from the classic Trek— the incomparable Mr. Spock (Leonard Nimoy, above), who along with his father Sarek (Mark Lenard, in his second appearance) makes a credible link from the Federation's past to its present. Makeup and costumes are used to great effect as Picard becomes the second Federation captain—Kirk was the first ("The Enterprise Incident")—to masquerade as a Romulan. Watch for Malachi Throne, who played Commodore Mendez in the classic Trek's "The Menagerie," as Senator Pardek. **Best scene:** *Sarek, on his deathbed, confiding to Picard his love for his ever-distant son.]*

UNIFICATION II
Week of Nov. 11, 1991, No. 207
STARDATE: 45245.8
Conclusion. After locating Spock (Leonard Nimoy) and discovering his plans for unifying the Romulans and the Vulcans, Picard and Data uncover a covert Romulan plot that does not call for unification— but for invasion. **Cmdr. Sela:** Denise Crosby. **Capt. K'Vada:** Stephen D. Root. **Senator Pardek:** Malachi Throne. **Proconsul Neral:** Norman Large. **Omag:** William Bastiani. **D'Tan:** Vidal Peterson. **Amarie:** Harriet Leider.

[Solid plot and great acting add to the suspense of this episode. And in a neatly writ-

ten bridge to an earlier plot line, the half-Romulan Cmdr. Sela (Denise Crosby in her fourth guest appearance) returns to cause trouble for the Federation. In a touching moment, Picard allows Spock to use the Vulcan Mind Meld to access the late Sarek's innermost feelings. **Best scene:** Data and Spock meet, allowing Data—whose desire to be human is still his fondest wish —to query the Vulcan as to why he chose instead to reject his humanity.]

A MATTER OF TIME
Week of Nov. 18, 1991, No. 209
STARDATE: 45349.1
While on a mission to save a planet that was hit by a huge asteroid, the Enterprise encounters a man (Matt Frewer) who claims to be from the future. **Dr. Hal Moseley:** Stefan Gierasch. **Ensign Felton:** Sheila Franklin. **Female Scientist:** Shay Garner.

[A light-hearted episode featuring Canadian actor Matt Frewer (Doctor, Doctor, Max Headroom). The part of the time-traveling Berlingoff Rasmussen was written for Robin Williams, who bowed out to star in "Hook."]

NEW GROUND
Week of Jan. 6, 1992, No. 210
STARDATE: 45376.3
On an unexpected visit, Worf's son (Brian Bonsall) delivers some startling news— he intends to take up permanent residence on the Enterprise. **Helena Rozhenko:** Georgia Brown. **Dr. Ja'Dar:** Richard McGonagle. **Kyle:** Jennifer Edwards. **Ensign Felton:** Sheila Franklin. **Computer Voice:** Majel Barrett.

[An episode that adds dimension to Worf's character as he struggles to become a father to Alexander (Brian Bonsall, "Blank Check," Family Ties), tapping unsuspected reserves of love and patience. Worf and Troi discover their common interest in Alexander and, for the first time—but not the last—in each other.]

HERO WORSHIP
Week of Jan. 27, 1992, No. 211
STARDATE: 45397.3
A young boy (Joshua Harris), the only survivor of a destroyed research vessel, becomes attached to Data (Brent Spiner) and attempts to emulate the android. **Transporter Chief:** Harley Venton. **Ensign Felton:** Sheila Franklin. **Teacher:** Steven Einspahr.

[In the second episode directed by Patrick Stewart, the crew again tends to a young orphan who, while understandably traumatized by the destruction of his ship and the loss of his parents, makes a friend in Data and begins to mimic his every move—in both humorous and poignant fashion. As Data and Troi struggle to reach Timothy, Geordi recalls his own terror at the deadly fire that nearly killed him when he was 5.]

VIOLATIONS
Week of Feb. 3, 1992, No. 212
STARDATE: 45429.3
Crew members begin to fall into inexplicable comas when the Enterprise plays host to a delegation of telepathic aliens. **Keiko O'Brien:** Rosalind Chao. **Jev:** Ben Lemon. **Tarmin:** David Sage. **Dr. Martin:** Rick Fitts. **Inad:** Eve Brenner. **Lt.- Cmdr. Jack Crusher:** Doug Wert. **Crewman Davis:** Craig Benton. **Computer Voice:** Majel Barrett.

[Frightening episode that takes physical assault one step further—into the mind. Before lapsing into comas, Troi, Riker and Crusher are repeatedly subjected to violent, horrifying memories, caused by the alien Jev, a telepathic violator posing as an historian. **Scariest scene:** Beverly is forced to peer into her husband's coffin, only to find Jev there waiting for her.]

THE MASTERPIECE SOCIETY
Week of Feb. 10, 1992, No. 213
STARDATE: 45470.1
Picard and the crew of the Enterprise work to save a genetically engineered society

from a natural disaster—but their efforts could be equally destructive. **Aaron Conor:** John Snyder. **Hannah Bates:** Dey Young. **Martin Benbeck:** Ron Canada. **Ensign Felton:** Sheila Franklin.

[A thought-provoking episode on genetic engineering with Troi and Geordi playing central roles in the debate. While Troi immediately regrets her brief, "genetically incorrect" affair with the human colony's leader, Geordi works to solve their engineering problem, knowing full well that, being blind, he would never have been allowed to live in their society.]

CONUNDRUM
Week of Feb. 17, 1992, No. 214
STARDATE: 45494.2
The crew of the Enterprise experiences complete memory loss and becomes engaged in a baffling battle with the Lysians. **Cmdr. Kieran MacDuff:** Erich Anderson. **Ensign Ro Laren:** Michelle Forbes. **Kristin:** Liz Vassey. **Crewman:** Erick Weiss.

[Intriguing glimpse at what might have been. Suffering complete memory loss, the crew begins to assume the identities that feel most comfortable to them: Worf decides he must be the captain of the Enterprise, while Picard becomes the navigator; Ro and Riker, meanwhile, find they share a mutual attraction.]

POWER PLAY
Week of Feb. 24, 1992, No. 215
STARDATE: 45571.2
Troi, Data and O'Brien stage a mutiny on board the Enterprise after investigating a strange distress signal originating from an apparently uninhabited moon. **Keiko O'Brien:** Rosalind Chao. **Miles O'Brien:** Colm Meaney. **Ensign Ro Laren:** Michelle Forbes. **Transporter Technician:** Ryan Reid. **Computer Voice:** Majel Barrett.

[Marina Sirtis, Brent Spiner and Colm Meaney get to step out of character when Troi, Data and O'Brien are possessed by disembodied entities, prisoners of an unsuspected penal colony located on the "uninhabited" moon.]

ETHICS

Week of March 2, 1992, No. 216
STARDATE: 45587.3
After Worf (Michael Dorn) is paralyzed in an accident, he is forced to choose between Klingon ritual suicide or experimental surgery. **Dr. Toby Russell:** Caroline Kava. **Alexander:** Brian Bonsall. **Nurse Alyssa Ogawa:** Patti Tasutake.

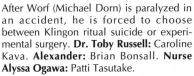

[A pair of ethical issues forces Worf and Dr. Crusher to reexamine their values, and places them in conflict with their colleagues. With his request for assistance in committing ritual suicide rejected by Riker, Worf turns to his son Alexander—but, in his reluctance to put his 7-year-old through the ordeal, he begins to question his Klingon resolve. Beverly, meanwhile, objects vehemently to Dr. Russell's determination to risk her patients' lives to prove her theories. Worf dies, for the second time, in surgery before his Klingon anatomy—featuring a backup synaptic system—kicks in to resuscitate him.]

THE OUTCAST
Week of March 16, 1992, No. 217
STARDATE: 45614.6
Riker becomes romantically involved with a member (Melinda Culea) of the J'naii —an androgynous race that prohibits male-female relationships. **Krite:** Callan White. **Noor:** Megan Cole.

[In one of the season's most controversial episodes, the issues of sexual preference and tolerance are put to the test. When Soren is put on trial for her involvement with Riker, the first officer assumes full responsibility while defending his lover's right to choose to be female. But, in a heart-wrenching scene, Riker must deal with the brainwashing cure she is forced

to undergo as punishment. Placing both himself and his career at risk, he attempts to rescue Soren only to have her renounce him as the brainwashing takes hold.]

CAUSE AND EFFECT
Week of March 23, 1992, No. 218
STARDATE: 45652.1
The Enterprise becomes trapped in a time warp, causing it to repeatedly experience the same fatal collision with another ship. **Ensign Ro Laren:** Michelle Forbes. **Nurse Alyssa Ogawa:** Patti Yasutake. **Capt. Morgan Bateman:** Kelsey Grammer.

[In the fourth episode directed by Jonathan Frakes, a sequence of events leading to the ship's destruction is repeated again and again, as the Enterprise falls into a time loop that steals 17 days out of the ship's history. Kelsey Grammer (above, Frasier, Cheers) has a letter-perfect cameo as the bemused Capt. Bateman of the other time-looped ship, which has been trapped for 90 years.]

THE FIRST DUTY
Week of March 30, 1992, No. 219
STARDATE: 45703.9
Prior to Starfleet Academy commencement ceremonies, an in-flight accident destroys five ships, including the one carrying Wesley Crusher (Wil Wheaton) and his

squadron. **Boothby:** Ray Walston. **Cadet First Class Nicholas Locarno:** Robert Duncan McNeill. **Lt.-Cmdr. Albert:** Ed Lauter. **Capt. Satelk:** Richard Fancy. **Supt. Admiral Brand:** Jacqueline Brookes. **Cadet Second Class Jean Hajar:** Walker Brandt. **Cadet Second Class Sito:** Shannon Fill.

[In Wil Wheaton's second guest appearance since leaving the series, Wesley comes of age when he realizes that loyalty to the truth—the first duty of a Starfleet officer, as Picard reminds him—is worth more than friendship, leading him to testify against his squadron after one of his team is killed during an ill-fated attempt at a banned flight manoeuvre. A first glimpse at Starfleet Academy, where Picard catches up with Boothby (Ray Walston, above, with Patrick Stewart), the Academy groundskeeper and his mentor.]

COST OF LIVING
Week of April 20, 1992, No. 220
STARDATE: 45733.6
Lwaxana (Majel Barrett) upsets Troi and Worf by taking Alexander (Brian Bonsall) under her wing; the Enterprise experiences mechanical problems when parasites attach themselves to the ship. **Campio:** Tony Jay. **Mr. Homn:** Carel Struycken. **Young Man:** David Oliver. **Juggler:** Albie Selznick. **Erko:** Patrick Cronin. **Young Woman:** Tracey D'Arcy. **Poet:** George Edie. **First Learner:** Christopher Halste.

[Another first-rate Lwaxana storyline—her fifth—delivering humor, conflict and near-disaster in equal measure. On board to be married to a man she hasn't met, the high-spirited Betazoid befriends Alexander—to the consternation of both Worf and Deanna—and teaches him something about life while learning a lesson of her own. Best scene: Lwaxana arrives at the ceremony in traditional Betazoid wedding attire—the nude—much to the embarrassment of her guests, not to mention her stuffy fiancé, who flees in panic.]

THE PERFECT MATE
Week of April 27, 1992, No. 221
STARDATE: 45761.3
The signing of a treaty between two warring races is complicated when Picard falls in love with the woman (Famke Janssen) who's serving as the peace offering. **Briam:** Tim O'Connor. **Par Lenor:** Max Grodenchik. **Alrik:** Mickey Cottrell. **Qol:** Michael Snyder. **Transporter Chief Hubble:** April Grace. **Computer Voice:** Majel Barrett.

[Bittersweet tale of true love lost, with Picard the unhappy protagonist. Interesting debate between the captain and Crusher as to whether Kamala's cultural obligations amount to prostitution, and whether the Federation has the right to interfere with those obligations on moral grounds. Kamala's spotted temples and hairline will later be seen on the host body of the Trill, Jadzia Dax, of Deep Space Nine.]

IMAGINARY FRIEND
Week of May 4, 1992, No. 222
STARDATE: 45832.1
The imaginary friend of a young girl Clara (Noley Thornton) comes to life when the Enterprise enters a section of space inhabited by a strange form of energy. **Isabella:** Shay Astar. **Ensign Daniel Sutter:** Jeff Allin. **Alexander:** Brian Bonsall. **Nurse Alyssa Ogawa:** Patti Yasutake. **Ensign Felton:** Sheila Franklin.

Guinan: Whoopi Goldberg.

I, BORG
Week of May 11, 1992, No. 223
STARDATE: 45854.2

The Away Team discovers an injured adolescent Borg (Jonathan Del Arco), whom they bring aboard the ship and nurse back to health, creating mixed emotions among the crew. **Guinan:** Whoopi Goldberg.

[In STNG's second most popular Borg episode among TV GUIDE readers, Dr. Crusher saves the life of an injured Borg, whom Geordi befriends and names Hugh. With the crew divided as to whether the young Borg should be saved or destroyed, Picard faces a critical decision as to whether he should return Hugh to the collective and expose the Federation to future risk—a decision whose consequences Picard will have to face in the sixth season's "Descent I." Jonathan Del Arco gives a riveting performance as the young Borg who learns to become an individual.]

THE NEXT PHASE
Week of May 18, 1992, No. 224
STARDATE: 45092.4
La Forge and Ro (LeVar Burton, Michelle Forbes) are assumed to be dead when they vanish during transport back to the Enterprise from a Romulan science ship. **Mirok:** Thomas Kopache. **Varel:** Susanna Thompson. **Transporter Chief Brossmer:** Shelby Leverington. **Parem:** Brian Cousins. **Ensign McDowell:** Kenneth Meseroll.

[Neat special effects, as Geordi and Ro —accidentally cloaked through Romulan chicanery—walk through walls as their crewmates walk through them. While Data searches for an appropriate memorial service by which to mark his comrades' deaths, we learn of different cultural traditions: for Worf, an honorable death is cause to celebrate, whereas Ro would prefer the two-hour Bajoran death chant for her borhyas, or soul. Jonathan Frakes

once again does his own trombone playing as Riker gets into the spirit of the Mardi Gras-style wake Data finally settles on.]

THE INNER LIGHT
Week of June 1, 1992, No. 225
STARDATE: 45944.1
After being hit by an emission from a primitive space probe, Picard finds himself living another man's life on a planet doomed by drought. **Eline:** Margot Rose. **Batai:** Richard Riehle. **Administrator:** Scott Jaeck. **Meribor:** Jennifer Nash. **Nurse Alyssa Ogawa:** Patti Yasutake. **Young Batai:** Daniel Stewart.

[In a wonderfully touching change-of-pace episode, Picard lives another man's life while under the influence of the space probe. As Kamin, an iron weaver on the planet Kataan, Picard has a wife, a loving relationship with his children, and a life-long—but, in the end, futile—mission to help save the planet from drought. As Kamin nears the end of his own life, the significance of the probe becomes clear: It was launched by the long-since dead Kataanians to record their story, and Picard was used as the witness through

which that story might be told. Having lived Kataan's demise through Kamin's eyes, Picard awakens on the Enterprise 25 minutes later a changed man—with Kamin's flute and the memories of that lifetime to carry forward in his own. Watch for Daniel Stewart—Patrick Stewart's son (with his father, left)—in the role of Batai, Kamin's son on Kataan.]

TIME'S ARROW I
Week of June 15, 1992, No. 226
STARDATE: 45959.1
An archeological dig on Earth uncovers an unusual 19th-century artifact—Data's head—and evidence of alien activity, leading the crew to San Francisco in the late 1800s to investigate. Part 1 of two. **Samuel Clemens:** Jerry Hardin. **Bellboy:** Michael Aron. **Doorman:** Barry Kivel. **Seaman:** Ken Thorley. **Joe Falling Hawk:** Sheldon P. Wolfchild. **Gambler/Frederick La Rouque:** Marc Alaimo. **Scientist:** Milt Tarver. **Guinan:** Whoopi Goldberg. **Roughneck:** Michael Hungerford. **Beggar:** John M. Murdock.

[Another season-ending cliffhanger with an intriguing twist: While searching for clues to the artifact, Data is sucked back in time to 1893 San Francisco—where he promptly meets Mark Twain (Clemens) and discovers a Guinan who does not recognize him, living as a wealthy socialite. Jerry Hardin is amusing as the irrepressible Samuel Clemens, who eavesdrops on Guinan and Data and earns himself a trip to the future. And, as the season ends, we're left to ponder: What ever happened to Data's head?]

ENCOUNTERS
PLANETS: Bilana III, Devidia II, Earth, Kataan, Krios, Lysia, Mab-Bu VI, Melona IV, Moab IV, Penthara IV, Romulus, Solarian IV
RACES: Bajorans, J'naii, Lysians, Kriosian, Sataarans, Tamarians, Ullians, Valtese
SHIPS: Bozeman, Essex, Vico

STAR TREK © 1994 PARAMOUNT PICTURES

Sixth Season

With rumors already circulating that *STNG*'s sixth season might well be its last, the year was marked by a number of storylines that brought closure to earlier episodes and a sense of completeness for several crew members, among them: Data, who, in seeking his father, meets again with his evil twin; Worf, who, in undertaking his own paternal quest, discovers the spiritual side to his Klingon nature; Riker, who discovers his long-lost other self and, in the process, gets a second chance to build a life with Deanna; and Picard, who journeys to the afterlife and is tempted to undo his past mistakes. And while, happily, Q returns in the sixth season to resume his mischief-making, Lwaxana Troi—another fan favorite—sadly does not. Still, it's a season of sentimental high notes—including the return of Lt.-Cmdr. Montgomery Scott to the Federation fold and the season-ending guest appearance of physicist Stephen Hawking. With the cast eventually signed to a seventh year, the sixth season would emerge as one of superb storytelling—stories that, while allowing the crew to seek out new life, would remind them, too, to seek within.

TIME'S ARROW II
Week of Sept. 21, 1992, No. 227
STARDATE: 46001.3
Conclusion. The Enterprise crew encounters parasitic time travelers and a suspicious Samuel Clemens (Jerry Hardin) during the search for Data in 19th-century San Francisco. **Guinan:** Whoopi Goldberg. **Mrs. Carmichael:** Pamela Kosh. **Young Reporter:** Alexander Enberg. **Morgue Attendant:** Van Epperson. **Dr. Appollinaire:** James Gleason. **Male Patient:** Bill Cho Lee. **Policeman:** William Boyett. **Alien Nurse:** Mary Stein. **Jack London:** Michael Aron.

[In the life-or-death conclusion to the fifth-season finale, we learn why Data's head—blown off in an explosion—was separated from his body in the first place. In the wake of Worf's miraculous fifth-season recovery, Data is the second crew member brought back from the dead. Picard, meanwhile, finally discovers how he really met Guinan, and the meddlesome Sam

Clemens earns a quick trip to the 24th century. Unlike other aliens in the Federation universe, the soul stealers of this episode are deemed evil, without being given the usual opportunity to redeem themselves.]

REALM OF FEAR
Week of Sept. 28, 1992, No. 228
STARDATE: 46091.1
A crewman's fear of being transported intensifies after he encounters a mysterious creature while transporting back to the Enterprise from a marooned ship. **Lieut. Barclay:** Dwight Schultz. **Admiral Hayes:** Renata Scott. **O'Brien:** Colm Meaney. **Nurse Ogawa:** Patti Yasutake. **Crew Member:** Thomas Velgrey. **Computer Voice:** Majel Barrett.

[Dwight Schultz makes his third appearance as the phobia-afflicted Barclay, who this time suffers from a well-justified fear of transporters. The hapless Barclay must overcome his fear to save his own life and the lives of four missing USS Yosemite crew

members. Interesting special effects when one of the larger shapeless beings bites Barclay just before he emerges from the transporter buffer.]
....

MAN OF THE PEOPLE
Week of Oct. 5, 1992, No. 229
STARDATE: 46071.6
While an alien ambassador (Chip Lucia) attempts to mediate a truce between two warring factions, Troi's behavior begins to change—as does her appearance. **Jarth:** Rick Scarry. **Maylor:** Susan French. **Ensign Janeway:** Lucy Boryer. **Admiral:** George D. Wallace. **Liva:** Stephanie Erb.

[Not the first Starfleet officer to undergo rapid aging (the original Trek's "The Deadly Years"), Troi is also subjected to a number of disturbing personality changes, seducing men at random, raging with jealousy and assaulting others. In a chilling discovery, Ambassador Alkar is found to be responsible for Troi's condition, having chosen her as the receptacle for his own negative emotions to free himself up to be the perfect diplomat—a condition he has repeatedly and remorselessly imposed on others. Deanna becomes the third crew member revived after her death. Watch for Worf to lead the Mak'bahr, a Klingon meditation exercise.]
....

RELICS
Week of Oct. 12, 1992, No. 230
STARDATE: 46125.3
After encountering the wreck of a starship that crashed 75 years ago, the Enterprise crew discovers a survivor suspended in the transporter system—Montgomery "Scotty" Scott (James Doohan). **Rager:** Lanei Chapman. **Kane:** Erick Weiss. **Engineer Bartel:** Stacie Foster. **Waiter:** Ernie Mirich. **Computer Voice:** Majel Barrett.

[A clever means to bring back a beloved character—the fourth—from the classic Trek. James Doohan (above) does a credible turn as the 147-year-old Scotty trying to

prove his usefulness in a society that's changed beyond recognition—which, given his resourcefulness, he does, of course. Best scene: The holodeck's re-creation of the original NCC-1701 bridge—background beeps and all. Best line: "Geordi, I've spent my whole life tryin' to figure out crazy ways to do things. I'm tellin' ya—one engineer to another—I can do this."]
....

SCHISMS
Week of Oct. 19, 1992, No. 231
STARDATE: 46154.2
When an experiment of La Forge's goes awry, the crew is subjected to an alien presence that causes people to suffer mysterious ailments—and to vanish from the ship. **Rager:** Lanei Chapman. **Mott:** Ken Thorley. **Shipley:** Scott Trost. **Crewman:** Angelo McCabe. **Kaminer:** Angelina Fiordellisi. **Medical Technician:** John Nelson. **Computer Voice:** Majel Barrett.

[Another just-in-the-nick-of-time solution by Geordi saves the crew and ship from the machinations of the antimatter aliens. Again the holodeck is used to great effect to re-create the terrifying recollections of the four crew members—Riker, Worf and Geordi among them—who were painfully cut apart and examined by the unfriendly aliens. Best scene: Data reads a comedic poem dedicated to his pet cat, Spot.]

TRUE Q
Week of Oct. 26, 1992, No. 232
STARDATE: 46192.3
While on a mission to save a polluted planet, a young intern (Olivia d'Abo) aboard the Enterprise displays unusual powers—and is visited by Picard's old foe Q. **Q:** John de Lancie. **Lote:** John P. Connolly.

[Finally, the sixth Q episode, as the troublesome alien shows up to train the interning Amanda, who is as surprised as the crew to discover herself to be the orphan daughter of two former members of the Q Continuum. Amanda's parents chose to leave the Continuum only to be killed by a freak tornado that struck their home in—are you ready?—Kansas. Under Q's guidance, Amanda turns out to be a precocious student, as Riker—every alien's favorite boy toy—is quick to discover. **Best scene:** *The 24th-century wizard is at his arrogant best when, explaining his possible need to terminate Amanda's life, Q tells Picard that it just wouldn't do to have omnipotent beings running around the universe. So what's his excuse?]*

RASCALS
Week of Nov. 2, 1992, No. 233
STARDATE: 46235.7
Picard, Guinan, Ensign Ro and Keiko are transformed into children during an unfortunate accident—which may prove fortunate to the Enterprise when it's seized by Ferengi. **Guinan:** Whoopi Goldberg. **Ensign Ro:** Michelle Forbes. **Keiko:** Rosalind Chao. **Berik:** Tracey Walter. **Morta:** Michael Snyder. **Alexander:** Brian Bonsall. **Young Picard:** David Tristan Birkin. **Young Guinan:** Isis Jones. **Young Keiko:** Caroline Junko King. **Lurin:** Mike Gomez. **O'Brien:** Colm Meaney. **Young Ro:** Megan Parlen. **Kid No. 1:** Morgan Nagler. **Molly:** Hana Hatae. **Computer Voice:** Majel Barrett.

[A neat reversal of the rapid-aging storyline, this episode was directed by Adam

Nimoy, Leonard Nimoy's son. Watch for David Tristan Birkin, who played nephew Rene Picard in the fourth season's "Family," in a return engagement as the 12-year-old Jean-Luc.]

A FISTFUL OF DATAS
Week of Nov. 9, 1992, No. 234
STARDATE: 46271.5
A holodeck adventure turns deadly for Worf and Alexander (Michael Dorn, Brian Bonsall), who find themselves pitted against two Wild West outlaws—both with Data's face and android abilities. **Annie:** Joy Garrett. **Bandito:** Jorge Cervera. **Eli Hollander:** John Pyper-Ferguson. **Computer Voice:** Majel Barrett.

[Patrick Stewart's third episode as director. Brent Spiner does a terrific job in five roles, playing nearly all the characters in Worf's holodeck melodrama—and has the last laugh when, transformed into a suspiciously robotic-looking Miss Annie, the fully functional android gets to put on "her" best show of gratitude when the mighty Klingon warrior saves the day.]

THE QUALITY OF LIFE
Week of Nov. 16, 1992, No. 235
STARDATE: 46307.2
Data is forced to choose between man and machine after a scientist (Ellen Bry) introduces the crew to devices know as "exocomps"—which he believes are alive. **Dr. Farallon:** Ellen Bry. **Transporter Chief Kelso:** David Windsor. **Computer Voice:** Majel Barrett.

[Fifth episode directed by Jonathan Frakes. Chalk one up for the android when, once again, Data correctly realizes that the Exocomps—like the Nanites of the third season—are sentient beings, and he stubbornly refuses to send them into danger, even under threat of court martial and with the captain's life at stake. **Best scene:** *Picard, having escaped with his life thanks to the Exocomps' decision to help, tells*

Data that his decision to fight for the Exocomps' rights was "the most human decision you've ever made."]

CHAIN OF COMMAND I
Week of Dec. 14, 1992, No. 236
STARDATE: 46357.4
As relations between the Federation and the Cardassians deteriorate, Picard resigns his command of the Enterprise to lead a secret mission with Worf and Crusher. Part 1 of two. **Capt. Jellico:** Ronny Cox. **Gul Lemec:** John Durbin. **Gul Madred:** David Warner. **Admiral Nechayev:** Natalija Nogulich. **Solok:** Lou Wagner.

[Picard is assigned a kamikaze mission to determine whether the Cardassians are manufacturing a metagenic weapon—the biological equivalent of a neutron bomb—as Capt. Jellico assumes command of the Enterprise in a transition that is anything but smooth for Jellico, Riker and the entire crew. Meanwhile, Picard, an expert in the theta-band subspace waves required by the weapon from his days in command of the USS Stargazer, leads a commando team consisting of himself, Worf and Dr. Crusher into the Cardassian installation on Celtris III, thought to be a metagenic production facility. The suspense mounts as the trio enters a Cardassian trap and Picard is captured. Part I ends as Picard—Serial No. SP-937-215—prepares to be interrogated. Watch for Troi to don a regulation Starfleet uniform at the request of Capt. Jellico.]

CHAIN OF COMMAND II
Week of Dec. 21, 1992, No. 237
STARDATE: 46360.8
Conclusion. While Picard is held captive and tortured by Gul Madred (David Warner), Capt. Jellico infuriates the crew with his callous behavior—and endangers the Enterprise by planning a first strike on the Cardassians. **Capt. Jellico:** Ronny Cox. **Gul Lemec:** John Durbin. **Jil Orra:** Heather Lauren Olson.

[Powerful conclusion, as Picard is brought to the brink of brainwashing by repeated torture. Patrick Stewart, who prepared for the demanding script by watching tapes provided by Amnesty International, gives a painfully accurate performance of a man punished again and again until he is very nearly driven into giving his warden anything he wants. Aboard the Enterprise, meanwhile, tension remains high as Data becomes acting first officer when Riker is relieved of his responsibilities for having questioned Jellico's judgment. In the end, of course, Jellico must ask for Riker's help in piloting the shuttle on a mission to plant mines on the Cardassian ships—the success of which leads to the Cardassian withdrawal and Picard's release. Not a moment too soon for Picard, who—as the shaken captain confides to Troi in the episode's final scene—was close to believing his torturer's taunts. The episode's Cardassian storyline provided a timely bridge to that of Deep Space Nine, which premièred in January 1993.]

SHIP IN A BOTTLE
Week of Jan. 25, 1993, No. 238
STARDATE: 46424.1
The game is afoot when a Sherlock Holmes holodeck adventure goes awry, releasing arch-nemesis Professor Moriarty (Daniel Davis) from the realm of computer simulation to reality. **Lieut. Barclay:** Dwight Schultz. **Countess:** Stephanie Beacham. **Gentleman:** Clement Von Franckenstein. **Computer Voice:** Majel Barrett.

[A light-hearted break from the serious episodes of recent weeks. In Dwight Schultz's fourth appearance, Lieut. Barclay accidentally releases Professor Moriarty from the holodeck program in which he was stored four years earlier ("Elementary, Dear Data"). Moriarty amazes himself and the entire crew when he appears to live and breathe outside the holodeck and, as before, seeks to gain control of the Enterprise. A neat mirror-within-a-mirror

episode, where one is never too sure what's real and what's imaginary. Watch for Daniel Davis (above left) as Moriarty and Stephanie Beacham (above right, seaQuest, DSV) as his beloved Countess Regina Bartholomew.]

AQUIEL
Week of Feb. 1, 1993, No. 239
STARDATE: 46461.3
Geordi (LeVar Burton) finds himself drawn romantically to a Starfleet lieutenant (Renee Jones) who is suspected of murder. **Lieut. Aquiel:** Renee Jones. **Torak:** Wayne Grace. **Morag:** Reg E. Cathey. **Computer Voice:** Majel Barrett.

[Geordi finally falls for a woman who returns his interest, only to have her accused of murder, in an episode tied to a Klingon storyline. But at least the loveless La Forge saves the day—and Aquiel's career—when he destroys the murderous alien blob masquerading as Aquiel's pet dog.]

FACE OF THE ENEMY
Week of Feb. 8, 1993, No. 240
STARDATE: 46519.1
The Romulan underground coerces Troi into impersonating a Romulan officer in a scheme to enable members of the senate to defect to the Federation. **N'Vek:** Scott MacDonald. **Toreth:** Carolyn Seymour. **DeSeve:** Barry Lynch. **Alien Captain:** Dennis Cockrum. **Pilot:** Robertson Dean.

[Another opportunity for a Starfleet officer—this time Troi, kidnapped for the second time—to go undercover as a Romulan. Marina Sirtis does an excellent job as the unwilling Troi, who has been surgically altered (above) to become Maj. Rakal of the Tal Shiar (the Romulan intelligence) and who, when her cover is threatened, is forced to assume command abilities or die. The episode provides an intriguing link to the covert diplomatic mission begun by Ambassador Spock in the fifth season's two-part "Unification."]

TAPESTRY
Week of Feb. 15, 1993, No. 241
STARDATE: Unknown
After Picard is mortally wounded during a surprise attack, he finds himself in the afterlife with his foe Q (John de Lancie), who gives him a chance to change his destiny. **Corey:** Ned Vaughn. **Marta:** J.C. Brandy. **Penny Muroc:** Rendé Rae Norman. **Nausicaan No. 1:** Clint Carmichael. **Maurice Picard:** Clive Church. **Young Picard:** Marcus Nash. **Computer Voice:** Majel Barrett.

[In his seventh episode, Q tempts Picard with a chance to undo his life's mistakes,

taking him back to the time when, as a 21-year-old ensign, he was stabbed through the heart by a Nausicaan in a bar fight. But Picard's refusal to be goaded a second time into the fight that cost him his heart—replaced surgically by an artificial one—costs him instead his passion, his courage, his friends and his captain's bars. Realizing that he would rather die like a man than play it safe, Picard asks Q for one more chance to put things back the way they were and quickly finds himself once again impaled on a Nausicaan blade. And, for once, Picard finds himself grateful to Q for showing him that the good and the bad of his past were essential to making him what he is. Thanks to Q, Picard is the fourth crew member to be returned from the dead.]

BIRTHRIGHT I
Week of March 8, 1993, No. 242
STARDATE: 46578.4
A layover on Deep Space Nine marks the beginning of adventures for Worf and Data, as each sets out on a quest to find his father. Part 1 of two. **L'Kor:** Richard Herd. **Dr. Bashir:** Siddig El Fadil. **Shrek:** James Cromwell. **Ba'el:** Jennifer Gatti. **Gi'ral:** Cristine Rose.

[In the first STNG episode to link up directly with Deep Space Nine, Data learns to dream, and Worf learns to fight his prejudices, as each begins a journey to find their fathers and their pasts. In Part 1, Data is the primary focus when, as the result of an accidental plasma shock, dream circuits—designed by Dr. Soong to be activated only when Data reached a certain level of awareness—kick in early. As the metaphorical bird of his dreams, Data is set free by his new knowledge, even as Worf is captured and held—along with 73 Klingon prisoners, survivors of the raid on Khitomer and their descendants—inside an unsuspected Romulan prisoner-of-war camp. Also in this episode, Worf begins to sport a more warrior-like pony-

tail. Data's new-found ability to dream—which allows him to meet his father for the second time—would be explored further in the seventh season's "Phantasms."]

BIRTHRIGHT II
Week of March 15, 1993, No. 243
STARDATE: 46759.2
Conclusion. Worf (Michael Dorn) is imprisoned in a Romulan camp where Klingons and Romulans appear to coexist in peace—a situation that he finds unbearable. **Ba'el:** Jennifer Gatti. **Gi'ral:** Cristine Rose. **L'Kor:** Richard Herd. **Tokath:** Alan Scarfe. **Shrek:** James Cromwell. **Toq:** Sterling Macer Jr.

[In Part 2, the focus shifts to Worf, who learns that, while his father did die at Khitomer, the survivors of that raid—whose existence the Klingon High Council refused to acknowledge—have lived ever since as docile, peaceful prisoners of the Romulans. Worf's shock turns to disgust as he realizes that the children of the once-mighty warriors know nothing of their heritage. While plotting his escape, Worf begins to train the offspring in the ways of a Klingon, teaching them the Mak'bahr—a meditation exercise that is at the basis of all Klingon fighting techniques—and telling them of Kahless, the greatest Klingon warrior. But even as he rouses the younger generation to challenge their fate and assert their freedom, Worf must also come to respect their parents' wish to remain as prisoners rather than return to the outside world, which would dishonor their families. Michael Dorn is superb as Worf struggles to come to terms with his father's past while leading the descendants of Khitomer to a free and more honorable future—swearing the young Klingons to secrecy over the camp's existence, in honor of their parents' sacrifice. And again, Picard will demonstrate his loyalty and respect for Worf in keeping that secret. Watch for the first Klingon kiss between Worf and Ba'el. And later this season, in "Rightful Heir," Worf will come face to face with the legendary Kahless.]

STARSHIP MINE
Week of March 29, 1993, No. 244
STARDATE: 46682.4
Picard (Patrick Stewart) is trapped aboard the Enterprise with a group of inter-galactic thieves after the rest of the crew evacuates the ship because of a dangerous cleaning process. **Kelsey:** Marie Marshall. **Hutchinson:** David Spielberg. **Devor:** Tim Russ. **Orton:** Glenn Morshower. **Kiros:** Patricia Tallman. **Neil:** Tom Nibley. **Satler:** Tim deZarn. **Waiter:** Arlee Reed. **Pomet:** Alan Altshuld.

[Another action episode for Stewart as Picard—who returns to the Enterprise to pick up his riding gear—discovers the ship taken over by a group of political terrorists out to steal trilithium resin for use as a weapon. Trapped alone with the terrorists as the deadly baryon sweep gets under way, Picard—who passes himself off as Mot, the ship's second-rate barber—works to booby trap their every escape route, leaving only Ten Forward as the final bat-tlefield. Unable to negotiate with Kelsey, the terrorists' leader—who has betrayed her comrades and is now stealing the resin for its commercial value—Picard plants a final booby trap by removing the resin's control rod and watches sadly as Kelsey's escaping ship explodes as a result. Watch for some early humorous moments as Data attempts to learn the art of small talk by imitating that of the all-too-dull Cmdr. Hutchinson.]

LESSONS
Week of April 5, 1993, No. 245
STARDATE: 46693.1
Picard (Patrick Stewart) falls in love with the new head of the ship's Stellar Sciences department (Wendy Hughes)—whom he must send on a dangerous mission.

[In an episode that provides a welcome change of pace and picks up the storyline begun in the fifth season's "The Inner Light," Picard falls into a relationship with Lt.-Cmdr. Nella Daren, sharing with her his love of music—gained on the planet Kataan—as well as his life there as Kamin. When Picard is called upon to send his new love on a life-threatening mission, the captain finds him-self—for the first time—torn between his personal feelings and his duty and sadly realizes that he cannot have one without risking the other. Watch for Australian actress Wendy Hughes (Homicide: Life on the Streets) in the role of Nella Daren.]

THE CHASE
Week of April 26, 1993, No. 246
STARDATE: 46731.5
Investigating an attack on his former archeology professor (Norman Lloyd), Picard tries to unravel a genetic mystery that may link the Cardassians, Klingons and Romulans. **Humanoid:** Salome Jens. **Nu'Daq:** John Cothran Jr. **Gul Ocett:** Linda Thorson. **Romulan Captain:** Maurice Roeves. **Professor Galen:** Norman Lloyd.

[Jonathan Frakes' sixth episode as director. A scientifically intriguing, action-packed episode that reunites Picard with Galen (Norman Lloyd, Dr. Auschlander in St. Elsewhere)—his archeology professor and mentor prior to his joining Starfleet—and pits the Enterprise against the Cardassians, Klingons and Romulans in a chase to uncover Galen's monumental discovery, the nature of which adds credence to the notion, first raised in the classic Trek's "The Paradise Syndrome," that the galaxy was genetically seeded by the same originat-ing species. First glimpse of a female Cardassian, Gul Ocett (Toronto-born Linda Thorson, The Avengers' Tara King).]

FRAME OF MIND
Week of May 3, 1993, No. 247
STARDATE: 46778.1
Riker (Jonathan Frakes) questions his sanity as he confronts altered realities—a theatrical presentation on the Enterprise, a covert mission and an alien insane asylum. **Dr. Syrus:** David Selburg. **Mavek:** Gary

Werntz. **Administrator:** Andrew Prine. **Inmate:** Susanna Thompson.

[A tour-de-force performance by Jonathan Frakes when, on a covert mission, Riker is captured and subjected to neural torture.]

SUSPICIONS
Week of May 10, 1993, No. 248
STARDATE: 46830.1
Dr. Crusher (Gates McFadden) jeopardizes her career as she investigates the death of a Ferengi scientist whose invention may have been coveted by others. **Kurak:** Tricia O'Neil. **Jo'Bril:** James Horan. **T'Pan:** Joan Stuart Morris. **Dr. Reyga:** Peter Slutsker. **Dr. Christopher:** John S. Ragin. **Ogawa:** Patti Yasutake. **Guinan:** Whoopi Goldberg.

[Gates McFadden is marvelous when Dr. Crusher—under threat of court martial—performs an illegal autopsy, relying on her judgment and stubborn determination to prove her suspicions of murder. The use of a shield strong enough to prevent the Enterprise from melting inside a star would resurface in the seventh season's "Descent II." Whoopi Goldberg also returns as Guinan, in only her third appearance this season. Watch for Tricia O'Neill, who played Capt. Rachel Garrett in "Yesterday's Enterprise," as the Klingon scientist Kurak.]

RIGHTFUL HEIR
Week of May 17, 1993, No. 249
STARDATE: 46852.2
A legendary Klingon warrior (Kevin Conway) returns to challenge Worf and threaten the stability of the High Council. **Koroth:** Alan Oppenheimer. **Gowron:** Robert O'Reilly. **Torin:** Norman Snow. **Divok:** Charles Esten. **Kahless:** Kevin Conway.

[In a powerful episode that has Worf searching for his Klingon spirituality—continuing the storyline begun in the two-part "Birthright"—Worf's faith is tested to the limit when he doubts, then believes, then doubts again that Kahless, the legendary Klingon warrior and true leader of the Klingon Empire, has actually returned. Discovering that this Kahless is in fact a clone of the original, Worf comes to realize that what matters is believing in the truth of Kahless' teachings rather than in Kahless himself. Resolved in the need to avert a new civil war, Worf forces Gowron to accept Kahless as spiritual leader and figurehead emperor, while leaving the secular power in the hands of Gowron and the High Council, of which Kurn, Worf's brother, is a member. Kahless, whose story was told in "Birthright II," was first seen in the classic Trek's "The Savage Curtain."]

SECOND CHANCES
Week of May 24, 1993, No. 250
STARDATE: 46915.2
During a visit to a former mission site, Riker (Jonathan Frakes) encounters his double—the result of a transporter mishap—and learns the man is still in love with Troi. **Ensign Palmer:** Dr. Mae Jemison (below left).

[In LeVar Burton's first episode as director, Jonathan Frakes does double duty as the Riker who serves aboard the Enterprise and the Will Thomas Riker who served eight years earlier on the USS Potemkin. The second Riker, created by a pair of transporter beams used to break through Nervala IV's distortion field, is as real as the first, but different in nature, and still in love with Deanna. For the second time, a Will Riker

proposes to Deanna, but this time Troi turns him down—realizing that this Riker, like the first, will renege on his promise. A neat twist to the Riker-Troi romance, as Thomas Riker, still a lieutenant, leaves to take up his new posting aboard the USS Gandhi. Watch for Dr. Mae Jemison— NASA science mission specialist and the first female African-American astronaut in space—in a cameo as Ensign Palmer.]

TIMESCAPE
Week of June 14, 1993, No. 251
STARDATE: 46944.2
Returning from a conference, Picard, Troi, Data and La Forge find the Enterprise and a Romulan Warbird motionless, stuck in time—and in mid-battle. **Romulan/ Alien:** Michael Bofshever.

[A second episode directed by Adam Nimoy, Leonard Nimoy's son, with a suspenseful and clever plot that has Picard and associates seeking to control the space-time continuum by first moving time backward and then forward to save the Enterprise from a deadly engine core breach.]

DESCENT I
Week of June 21, 1993, No. 252
STARDATE: 46982.1
While investigating a Federation outpost massacre, the Enterprise encounters the Borg, whose individual identities and viciousness trigger a startling change in Data (Brent Spiner). Part 1 of two. **Professor Stephen Hawking:** Himself. **Isaac Newton:** John Neville. **Albert Einstein:** Jim Norton. **Crosis:** Brian J. Cousins. **Admiral Nechayev:** Natalija Nogulich.

[The second season-ender to feature the Borg (and their fifth episode). Picard must face the consequences of his earlier decision to return Hugh to the collective ("I, Borg")—in which a startling shift toward "individual" personalities seems to have occurred. And in an even more surprising development, Data kills out of anger, a feel-

ing—like all other feelings—thought to be impossible for his android circuitry. Taunted by a Borg prisoner, Data confirms the pleasure he felt in killing and admits that he would kill even Geordi, if it meant he could feel again what he felt before. With that, Data frees the Borg, and together they head for a planet that may have fallen to the collective. In pursuit, Picard leads an Away Team to the planet and straight into a Borg ambush—led not by Hugh, as Picard had feared, but by Lore, Data's evil twin. There he is joined by Data, who, in a chilling voice, promises that "The sons of Soong have joined together—and together, we will destroy the Federation," as the season comes to a heart-stopping end. Watch for the opening scene featuring world-renowned physicist Stephen Hawking (above) in a cameo as himself—a player in a holodeck-created poker game with Sir Isaac Newton (Canadian John Neville), Albert Einstein and Data.]

ENCOUNTERS
PLANETS: Bersallis III, Boreth, Celtris III, Devidia II, Draken IV, Indri VIII, Minos Korva, Nervala IV, Ohniaka III, Tilonus IV
RACES: Cardassians, Klingons, Lenarians, Nausicaans, Romulans
SHIPS: Ajax, Dorian, Jenolen, Yosemite

Seventh Season

As the seventh season began, the family reemerged as *STNG*'s most dominant theme, with several episodes bringing to full circle storylines begun in the fourth season. But where earlier seasons had explored the relationships of several crew members with their fathers, the seventh would turn itself to their mothers—Geordi's, Data's and Deanna's, in particular. Meanwhile, on the romantic front, two simmering relationships—that of Picard and Crusher, and that of Troi and Worf—were at last given new spark. In matters scientific, the year would also be marked by a number of clever episodes—one of which would allow Gates McFadden to make her directorial debut—based both on fact and intriguing possibility. But all good things must come to an end—as the title of *STNG*'s last episode would suggest. When, in early November, Paramount confirmed that the seventh season would be the last, the series that was always about so much more than phasers and warp speed began to tie up its loose ends. And while setting the stage for the next TV series—*Star Trek: Voyager*—*STNG* finished its run in the same position in which it had begun: the No. 1 hourlong drama in syndication.

DESCENT II
Week of Sept. 20, 1993, No. 253
STARDATE: 47025.4
Data, under the influence of his evil brother Lore, imprisons Picard, Troi and La Forge among the Borg. Meanwhile, the Enterprise, commanded by Dr. Crusher, comes under attack. **Hugh:** Jonathan Del Arco. **Taitt:** Alex Datcher. **Barnaby:** James Horan. **Crosis:** Brian J. Cousins.

[With Lore in control of both Data and the Borg, the sons of Soong begin to make good their threat, as the Enterprise, under Dr. Crusher's command, effects its escape. Back on the planet, Data—who has learned to feel anger and hate—subjects Geordi to dangerous neurological experiments at Lore's urging. Realizing that Lore has dismantled Data's ethical program, Geordi, Picard and Troi struggle to reactivate it by means of a crudely rigged kedion pulse. As the tension mounts, the action shifts to Riker and Worf, who are captured by a second group of Borg, led by the now bitter Hugh. Meanwhile, using only the ship's metaphasic shields for protection, Beverly orders the Enterprise to fly directly into the sun's corona as the crew devises a dangerous plan to destroy the Borg ship by creating a solar fusion eruption. With Geordi's kedion pulse beginning to take effect, Lore orders his brother to prove his loyalty by killing Picard. Data refuses, and just as Lore turns to kill his twin, Hugh—who has led Riker and Worf to the Borg compound out of friendship for Geordi—steps forward to knock the weapon from Lore's hand. As the Borg's sixth and final episode concludes, Data is forced to fire on the escaping Lore, whom he then deactivates, while Hugh becomes the Borg group's new leader. Watch for terrific special effects as the Enterprise blows the Borg ship away with a refractive shot into the sun.]

LIAISONS
Week of Sept. 27, 1993, No. 254
STARDATE: Unknown
The crew hosts Iyaaran ambassadors: One is assigned to Troi; the other seeks to provoke an undiplomatic Worf. Meanwhile, Picard, en route to Iyar, is rescued by a woman (Barbara Williams) who falls in love with him. **Voval:** Eric Pierpoint. **Loquel:** Paul Eiding. **Byleth:** Michael Harris.

[While Worf learns a valuable lesson in diplomacy, Picard teaches his own lesson in love, as Anna—the apparent sole survivor of a Terellian cargo freighter crash seven years earlier—is not what she appears to be.]

INTERFACE
Week of Oct. 4, 1993, No. 255
STARDATE: 47215.5
Geordi (LeVar Burton), attached to an experimental interfacing probe, thinks he sees his mother (Madge Sinclair) on a stranded ship—although the craft was reported missing more than three hundred light years away. **Admiral Holt:** Warren Munson. **Dr. La Forge:** Ben Vereen.

[LeVar Burton turns in a fine performance as Geordi risks his life and career in a desperate search for his mother, Capt. Silva La Forge—whose ship, the USS Hera, has disappeared without a trace—defying both his father and his captain to do so. Using an interface unit—a type of virtual reality device—Geordi appears to find his mother aboard the USS Raman, a science vessel trapped inside the turbulent atmosphere of an unusually gaseous planet. Though shocked to discover an alien masquerading as Silva La Forge, Geordi makes a courageous decision to risk his life to save the life forms who will die if not returned to the planet's lower atmosphere. Geordi revives from his life-threatening interface to face an angry Picard, and the episode concludes as Geordi realizes that his experience with his "alien" mother helped him say goodbye.]

GAMBIT I
Week of Oct. 11, 1993, No. 256
STARDATE: 47135.2
While investigating the apparent death of Capt. Picard, Riker is kidnapped and taken to a mercenary ship that's been looting archeological sites—only to discover Picard among the crew. Part 1 of two. **Baran:** Richard Lynch. **Tallera:** Robin Curtis. **Vekor:** Caitlin Brown. **Narik:** Cameron Thor. **Yranac:** Alan Altshuld. **Admiral Chekote:** Bruce Gray.

[In the fast-paced two-part adventure, Picard's interest in archeology leads to his fifth abduction, this time by mercenaries, searching for a number of mysterious and highly dangerous artifacts, who are out to loot the archeological site Picard is studying.]

GAMBIT II
Week of Oct. 18, 1993, No. 257
STARDATE: 47160.1
Conclusion. Picard and Riker, having integrated themselves with the mercenaries, seek to drive them to mutiny—and learn the true nature of the mysterious artifacts they seek. **Baran:** Richard Lynch. **Tallera:** Robin Curtis. **Vekor:** Caitlin Brown. **Narik:** Cameron Thor. **Koral:** James Worthy. **Ensign Giusti:** Sabrina LeBeauf.

[Intrigue and conspiracy abound as the search for the final artifact—believed to be Romulan—leads the mercenaries to rendezvous with a Klingon transport ship that leads, in turn, to a high-tempo chase back to the Enterprise. The chase becomes a race to the finish to prevent disaster when the artifacts turn out to be Vulcan in origin, fragments of the mythical Stone of Gol—a psionic resonator that, when reassembled, focuses and amplifies telepathic thought and is powerful enough to eliminate the entire Vulcan council in a single thought. Watch for L.A. Laker James Worthy as Koral—who, at 6-foot-9, is surely the tallest Klingon roaming the galaxy.]

PHANTASMS
Week of Oct. 26, 1993, No. 258
STARDATE: 47225.7
Data's dream program begins to produce nightmares that dangerously affect his behavior—but that may hold clues to unusual occurrences aboard the ship. **Ensign Tyler:** Gina Ravarra. **Sigmund Freud:** Bernard Kates. **Admiral Nakamura:** Clyde Kusatsu. **Workman:** David L. Crowley.

[Patrick Stewart's fourth episode as director. As Data pursues the dream state he experienced in "Birthright I," symbolic metaphors replace reality when Data can't stop dreaming about violent images. Watch for great special effects in Data's dream sequences as Deanna's shoulder gets sliced up like a piece of cake and Data reaches into his own stomach to answer a ringing phone.]

DARK PAGE
Week of Nov. 1, 1993, No. 259
STARDATE: 47254.1
Troi's mother, Lwaxana (Majel Barrett), suffers a breakdown while the Enterprise hosts a delegation of telepathic aliens. **Maques:** Norman Large. **Hedril:** Kirsten Dunst. **Ian Andrew Troi:** Amick Byram.

[In her sixth appearance, Majel Barrett delivers an intensely dramatic performance as Lwaxana Troi, suffering from repressed memory syndrome, collapses into a coma. Aided by Maques, one of the telepathic Cairn, Deanna enters her mother's mind and is confronted by a series of barriers sent by Lwaxana to prevent her daughter from going any further—including the image of her late father, who pleads with her to stay with him and whose urging Deanna tearfully resists. On a second incursion into her mother's mind, Troi is shocked to encounter Kestra—the sister she never knew she had, whose accidental death at age 7 has been a repressed memory for Lwaxana ever since. One of STNG's saddest episodes, as Deanna must fight to save her mother's life.]

ATTACHED
Week of Nov. 8, 1993, No. 260
STARDATE: 47304.2
Picard and Dr. Crusher discover their true feelings toward each other via a telepathic link when they become imprisoned together during a diplomatic mission. **Mauric:** Robin Gammell. **Lorin:** Lenore Kasdorf.

[The seventh episode directed by Jonathan Frakes. Forced together by telepathic link, Picard and Crusher finally explore the attraction that has simmered between them. After the captain explains that his love for Beverly was the real reason he did not want her assigned to the Enterprise seven years earlier, Picard suggests they pursue their relationship. This time, it's Beverly's turn to admit she's not yet ready.]

FORCE OF NATURE
Week of Nov. 15, 1993, No. 261
STARDATE: 47310.2
While searching for a missing ship, the Enterprise encounters an alien brother and sister who insist that warp-drive engines are destroying their region of outer space. **Rabal:** Michael Corbett. **Serova:** Margaret Reed. **Prak:** Lee Arenberg.

[In a thought-provoking storyline on the potential for advanced technologies to damage the environment, Picard and Geordi come to realize that by exploring the universe they love they may have inadvertently been contributing to its destruction. Issuing a new directive, the Federation Council limits all Federation vessels to a speed of Warp 5, except in emergency.]

INHERITANCE
Week of Nov. 22, 1993, No. 262
STARDATE: 47410.2
Data (Brent Spiner) meets a woman (Fionnula Flanagan) who claims to be Juliana Soong—Noonian Soong's ex-wife and Data's mother. **Pran:** William Lithgow.

[In the third episode this season to deal with the mother of a crew member, Data gets to complete his family circle with the appearance of Juliana Tainer, remarried since her divorce from Data's father, Noonian Soong. When Data learns that he was deactivated and intentionally left behind on Omicron Theta because Juliana feared that he would become evil like Lore, he begins to wonder whether Juliana would have abandoned him had he been her biological child. But when he discovers that Juliana is also an android—created after the Crystalline Entity killed the real Juliana—Data learns a lesson in compassion as the pleading image of Dr. Soong begs him not to tell Juliana the truth about her android self.]

PARALLELS
Week of Nov. 29, 1993, No. 263
STARDATE: 47391.2
Worf (Michael Dorn) finds he is the only one who notices reality changing—and his sanity ebbing—after he returns from a Klingon competition. **Ogawa:** Patti Yasutake. **Gul Nador:** Mark Bramhall. **Wesley:** Wil Wheaton.

[Wil Wheaton's third guest appearance since leaving the regular cast in the fourth season. This clever episode brings back the theme of parallel universes, this time with Worf as the very confused protagonist, who—while he unknowingly jumps from one universe into the next—hears Troi tell him that she's his wife and the mother of his two children. The episode features terrific special effects as Worf, attempting to return to his rightful universe by flying his shuttlecraft through a time rift in space, encounters dozens of others Worfs doing the same thing, and thousands of Enterprises. **Most unsettling scene:** A desperate Riker begs not to be sent back to his universe, which has been overtaken by the Borg, and decides instead to self-destruct his ship.]

THE PEGASUS
Week of Jan. 10, 1994, No. 264

STARDATE: 47457.1
Riker's loyalties are divided when his former commanding officer (Terry O'Quinn) risks the Enterprise on a dangerous mission to salvage his former ship. **Admiral Blackwell:** Nancy Vawter.

[A high-tension episode, LeVar Burton's second as director. Jonathan Frakes gives another terrific performance as Riker must weigh loyalty to his first captain—now Admiral Pressman—and loyalty to Picard. Twelve years earlier, the Pegasus—Riker's first assignment after leaving Starfleet Academy—was lost with most of its crew, the result of Pressman's deployment of an experimental device. When that turns out to be a prototype for a cloaking device that allows ships to travel through solid rock—a technology banned by Federation treaty—Picard learns from Riker that its use aboard the Pegasus led to mutiny by the crew and disaster for the ship. **Best scene:** Having been sealed into an asteroid by the Romulans—who are also searching for the prototype—the Enterprise uses the banned device to phase through the asteroid and escape, much to the surprise of the Romulan Warbird waiting on the other side.]

HOMEWARD
Week of Jan. 17, 1994, No. 265
STARDATE: 47423.9
On a mission to a planet that is losing its atmosphere, Worf encounters his adoptive brother (Paul Sorvino)—who violates the Prime Directive in a desperate attempt to save the inhabitants. **Dobara:** Penny Johnson. **Vorin:** Brian Markinson. **Kateras:** Edward Penn.

[Another fine episode focusing on the Prime Directive as the Enterprise responds to a distress call from Nikolai Rozhenko (Paul Sorvino, in a terrific guest appearance), Worf's foster brother and a cultural observer on Boraal II. The episode provides an interesting commentary on loyalty to one's family as Worf discovers that Nikolai is not only *trying to save the Boraalan people but also the Boraalan mother of his unborn child. Watch for Michael Dorn, minus his usual Klingon makeup, as Worf beams to the planet disguised as a Boraalan.]*

SUB ROSA
Week of Jan. 31, 1994, No. 266
STARDATE: Unknown
After Dr. Crusher (Gates McFadden) attends her grandmother's funeral, strange happenings lead her to believe she's inherited the family ghost. **Maturin:** Michael Keenan. **Ned Quint:** Shay Duffin. **Ronin:** Duncan Regehr.

[In this haunting story—Jonathan Frakes' eighth episode as director—Beverly's background and family history are more fully explored as she travels to Caldos IV to attend the funeral of her maternal grandmother, Felisa Howard. There she finds passion and love with Ronin (Duncan Regehr, V, Zorro), an apparent ghost who's loved the women in Beverly's family for over 800 years. But as Crusher resigns her post on the Enterprise, she discovers that Ronin is, in fact, an anaphasic life form that has been using the women in her family to stay alive. Gates McFadden delivers a splendid portrayal of a woman in the agonizing position of having to kill her lover when she realizes he means to kill her crewmates.]

LOWER DECKS
Week of Feb. 7, 1994, No. 267
STARDATE: 47566.7
Four junior officers find themselves tested beyond their expectations when a secret mission takes the place of their promotion evaluation. **Sam Lavelle:** Dan Gauthier. **Sito Jaxa:** Shannon Fill. **Taurik:** Alexander Enberg. **Ben:** Bruce Beatty. **Ogawa:** Patti Yasutake. **Joret:** Don Reilly.

[An intriguing episode that provides an understanding of what life as a young officer might have been like for Picard or Riker.]

THINE OWN SELF
Week of Feb. 14, 1994, No. 268
STARDATE: 47611.2
Data (Brent Spiner) finds himself stranded on a planet with a preindustrial society—with no memory of who he is or how he got there. Meanwhile, Troi takes the Bridge Officer's test. **Talur:** Ronnie Claire Edwards. **Garvin:** Michael Rothhaar. **Gia:** Kimberly Cullum. **Skoran:** Michael G. Hagerty.

[Data learns the meaning of friendship—as well as its power to overcome ignorance and fear—when, in a state of amnesia, he is befriended by a young girl and her father over the objections and threats of the other villagers. Data risks his own life to save them all from the radiation poisoning he inadvertently caused. Meanwhile, Deanna Troi faces her own test of strength when, to pass the Bridge Officer's test, she must knowingly send a crew member to his death.]

MASKS
Week of Feb. 21, 1994, No. 269
STARDATE: 47615.2
After the Enterprise encounters a mysterious comet, Data (Brent Spiner) exhibits multiple personalities, and the ship is transformed into an ancient city.

[In another extraordinary performance, Brent Spiner plays all of the alien personalities discovered in the ancient archive, as Data develops the android equivalent of multiple-personality syndrome.]

EYE OF THE BEHOLDER
Week of Feb. 28, 1994, No. 270
STARDATE: 47622.1
During the investigation of a crew member's mysterious suicide, Troi and Worf (Marina Sirtis and Michael Dorn) find their relationship taking a romantic turn. **Walter Pierce:** Mark Rolston. **Lieut. Nara:** Nancy Harewood. **Lieut. Kwan:** Tim Lounibos. **Calloway:** Johanna McCloy.

[In an episode that begins with suicide, then leads to murder and back to suicide, Troi and Worf conduct an investigation into events that occurred eight years earlier during the construction of the Enterprise at the Utopia Planitia Fleet Yards. The episode allows Troi to explore the attraction between her and Worf that began in the fifth season's "New Ground."]

GENESIS
Week of March 21, 1994, No. 271
STARDATE: 47653.2
The crew begins to exhibit strange behavioral changes—eventually regressing into primitive creatures. **Ogawa:** Patti Yasutake. **Barclay:** Dwight Schultz.

[Gates McFadden's directorial debut marks Dwight Schultz's fifth guest appearance as Lieut. Barclay. And if ever there were an episode to make the viewer wonder how Starfleet's finest were going to get out of this one, this is it. Makeup is used to great effect to turn Deanna into an amphibian, Riker into a prehistoric man, Worf into an early Klingon and Barclay into a half-man, half-spider. As Data races to find a cure to the virus that is causing the crew to de-evolve, Picard—

STAR TREK © 1994 PARAMOUNT PICTURES

who was away from the Enterprise when the virus first took hold—begins to feel unfamiliar pangs of fear and panic as he, too, begins to de-evolve, leading to an extraordinary scene as the captain is chased through the bowels of the Enterprise by a venom-spitting Worf (below). Fast action, eerie effects and a rather neat conclusion (thanks to a clue left by Spot, Data's pregnant cat) as the virus is traced back to a synthetic T-cell given to hypochondriac Barclay, for whom the disease—Barclay's Protomorphosis Syndrome—is then named.]

JOURNEY'S END
Week of March 28, 1994, No. 272
STARDATE: 47751.2
Wesley (Wil Wheaton), on a break from Starfleet Academy, becomes involved in a dispute over the relocation of native Americans from a planet annexed by the Cardassians. **Lakanta:** Tom Jackson. **Admiral Necheyev:** Natalija Nogulich. **Anthwara:** Ned Romero. **Wakasa:** George Aguilar. **Gul Evek:** Richard Poe. **Traveler:** Eric Menyuk. **Jack Crusher:** Doug Wert.

[Wil Wheaton returns in his fourth guest appearance as Wesley, unhappy at the Academy, stumbles on to his true destiny. Meanwhile, Picard is challenged to reverse a stain of blood worn by his family for 23 generations. Watch for Canadian Tom Jackson (North of 60) in the role of Lakanta, and the return of Eric Menyuk as the Traveler and Doug Wert as Jack Crusher.]

FIRSTBORN
Week of April 25, 1994, No. 273
STARDATE: 47779.4
Worf (Michael Dorn) must accept the fact that Alexander (Brian Bonsall) is destined to become a diplomat, not a warrior. **Lursa:** Barbara March. **B'Etor:** Gwynyth Walsh. **Yog:** Joel Swetow. **Gorta:** Colin Mitchell. **Eric:** Ricky D'Shon Collins. **Molor:** John Shull. **Singer:** Michael Danek. **K'Mtar:** James Sloyan. **Quark:** Armin Shimerman.

[Worf's family storyline continues. Armin Shimerman returns as Quark, his third and best-known Ferengi role, as the Enterprise makes its second stopover at Deep Space Nine. Watch for James Sloyan (who played Romulan Admiral Jarok in the third season's "The Defector") as the Klingon K'Mtar—who turns out to be none other than a grown-up Alexander, who has traveled from the future to save his father, Worf, from murder.]

....

BLOODLINES

Week of May 2, 1994, No. 274
STARDATE: 47829.1
A renegade Ferengi (Lee Arenberg) swears revenge on Picard—by killing the son (Ken Olandt) the captain never knew he had. **Birta:** Peter Slutsker.

[Tampering with evidence as he did in the first season's "The Battle," DaiMon Bok returns to exact vengeance on Picard for the death of Bok's son years earlier at the Battle of Maxia. But Bok's plans go awry when, having resequenced Jason Vigo's DNA to match Picard's, his duplicity is discovered and, for the second time, his Ferengi shipmates turn against him.]

....

EMERGENCE

Week of May 9, 1994, No. 275
STARDATE: 47869.2
The lives of the Enterprise crew are endangered when the ship suddenly develops its own intelligence. **Conductor:** David Huddleston. **Hitman:** Vinny Argiro. **Engineer:** Thomas Kopache. **Hayseed:** Arlee Reed.

[The holodeck is put to clever use in an imaginative episode in which the Enterprise actually gives birth to a new life form.]

....

THE GOOD FIGHT

Week of May 16, 1994, No. 276
STARDATE: 47941.7
When a group of vigilantes known as the Maquis threatens the Cardassian-Federation Demilitarized Zone, the Enterprise is ordered to protect a Cardassian convoy. **Ro Laren:**

Michelle Forbes. **Gul Evek:** Richard Poe. **Kalita:** Shannon Cochran. **Macias:** John Franklyn-Robbins. **Santos:** William Thomas Jr.

[Fifth episode directed by Patrick Stewart. Michelle Forbes makes her eighth appearance as Ro Laren, who returns to the Enterprise after completing Starfleet's Advanced Tactical Training, only to be assigned to join the Maquis as an undercover operative. But as the Bajoran begins to sympathize with the vigilantes' cause, she's forced to choose between them and her loyalty to Picard and the Federation. The Maquis, introduced in the two-part DS9 episode of the same name, will play a prominent role in Star Trek: Voyager.*]*

....

ALL GOOD THINGS...

Week of May 23, 1994, No. 747
STARDATE: 47988.0
Picard's arch-nemesis Q (John de Lancie) returns to put the captain on trial for the crimes of mankind. **Tasha Yar:** Denise Crosby. **O'Brien:** Colm Meaney.

[In the two-hour series finale, Q, in his eighth appearance, is back where he started—putting Picard on trial, as he did seven years earlier, and taking him on a quantum leap through the past, present and 25 years into the future. Familiar faces abound in an episode that brings closure to the USS Entreprise NCC-1701-D's very first encounter. The finale will repeat as two one-hour segments (Nos. 277, 278). And watch for the crew's next mission—"Star Trek: Generations"—coming in November to a theatre near you.]

ENCOUNTERS

PLANETS: Atrea, Barkon IV, Barradas III, Boraal II, Calder II, Caldos IV, Dorvan V, Kesprytt, Maranga IV, Vacca Six
RACES: Boraalans, Cairn, Iyaaran, Kes, Prytt, Yridians
SHIPS: Fleming, Hera, Pegasus, Raman

Fan Clubs

Wherever Trekkers gather, fan clubs are sure to follow. In North America, clubs number in the dozens and range in size from a few enthusiasts to thousands. Some follow every aspect of the *Star Trek* universe, while others dedicate themselves to a particular theme or character. Only two, however—the Official *Star Trek* Fan Club of Canada and *Star Trek: The Official Fan Club* (see boxes)—are officially sanctioned by Paramount and have direct access to the latest information, photography, interviews and collectibles. In addition, several clubs are recognized by the actor to whom they are dedicated or as local chapters of larger clubs. Below, we've provided the names, addresses and particulars of the most well-established clubs in Canada and the U.S.

Canadian Clubs

THE OFFICIAL STAR TREK FAN CLUB OF CANADA
77 MOWAT AVE., SUITE 621
TORONTO, ONT. M6K 3E3
(416) 538-1000 (FAX: 538-0201)
Officially Recognized: Yes
Established: February 1992
Membership Fee: $22.99
Includes: Card, jacket patch, trading cards, letter, four magazines
Meetings: No
Current Membership: 10,500

[For additional information, see inside back cover.]

ASTRAL ALLIANCE
605-580 CHRISTIE ST.
TORONTO, ONT. M6G 3E3
(416) 651-6779
Established: July 1993
Dedicated to: All aspects of science fiction, fantasy and new age philosophy
Name: Astral plane, the theoretical dimension that touches all realities
Membership Fee: $15 annually
Meetings: Monthly
Includes: Bimonthly newsletter
Current Membership: 12

CANADA SPACE STATION—STARFLEET INTERNATIONAL
44 SCENIC RD. N.W.
CALGARY, ALTA. T3L 1B9
(403) 239-4207
Recognized: Chapter of Starfleet International
Established: 1980
Name: An international club with chapters named after original ships in the "Star Trek Technical Manual"
Membership Fee: $20 US
Includes: Newsletter, membership card, memo pad, listing of worldwide chapters
Meetings: Twice monthly; annual *ST* convention in Calgary
Current Membership: 80 locally; 7000 worldwide

EXCALIBUR—OTTAWA STAR TREK CLUB
1068 BATHGATE DR.
GLOUCESTER, ONT. K1J 8E8
(613) 749-3436
Established: 1978
Name: Named after King Arthur's sword and a ship in the classic *Trek*
Membership Fee: $9

Includes: Newsletter and meetings
Current Membership: 40

IMPERIAL KLINGON BATTLE FLEET (INTERNATIONAL)
105 OAKDALE DR.
OAKVILLE, ONT. L6H 1J4
(905) 845-4288
Established: 1990
Dedicated to: Klingons on *STNG* but *will* associate with Romulans, Cardassians, Borg and Ferengi
Membership Fee: None, but all members are required to have a uniform
Meetings: Participates in 300 North American events a year—conventions, parades, trade and hobby shows and charitable events
Current Membership: Over 2000

THE KLINGON ASSAULT GROUP OF KANADA—KAG KANADA
31 HASTINGS AVE.
UNIONVILLE, ONT. L3R 3Y5
(905) 475-9343 (FAX: 905-453-2817)
Established: 1990 (in Canada)
Dedicated to: Klingons
Name: Chosen to project the correct Klingon image of toughness and aggression
Membership Fee: None
Includes: Quarterly newsletter $12
Meetings: Weekly or monthly; conventions, community and charitable events
Current Membership: Over 300 in Canada; over 1200 worldwide

KLINGON IMPERIAL DIPLOMATIC CORPS—KAG KANADA
1025 EVERETT ST., SUITE 2
MONTREAL, QUE. H2R 1N1
(514) 276-2406
Recognized: By KAG Kanada
Established: 1991
Dedicated to: Klingons and *STNG*
Name: Public relations arm of KAG Kanada
Membership Fee: None
Includes: Newsletter, ID card, nametag
Meetings: Community and charitable events; diplomatic receptions at conventions

Current Membership: Over 300 (KAG Kanada)

OUTPOST PHOENIX—INTERNATIONAL FEDERATION OF TREKKERS
#1-739 UNIVERSITY AVE. W.
WINDSOR, ONT. N9A 5R8
(519) 945-6321
Recognized: Chapter of International Federation of Trekkers (see U.S. listing)
Established: June 1, 1984
Name: Originated in Ohio but expanded to Canada
Membership Fee: $11 US ($3 each for additional family members)
Includes: IFT membership certificate, ID card, stardate chart, newsletter
Meetings: Chapter meetings in the U.S.; none in Canada
Current Membership: Over 1500

STARFLEET CANADA
P.O. BOX 22188, BANKERS HALL
CALGARY, ALTA. T2P 4J5
Established: 1988
Name: Chapter of Starfleet USA
Membership Fee: $10
Includes: Four magazines, membership card, handbook, certificate
Meetings: Last Wednesday of month
Current Membership: 125 worldwide

STAR TREK ASSOCIATION OF REGINA (STAR)
P.O. BOX 36007
REGINA, SASK. S4S 7H6
(306) 569-3729
Established: January 1992
Dedicated to: *Star Trek* and science fiction
Membership Fee: $20
Includes: Monthly newsletter and membership card
Meetings: Monthly meetings, video nights, several special events per year
Current Membership: 80

STAR TREK TORONTO, INC.
SUITE 0116, BOX 208
65 FRONT ST. W.

TORONTO, ONT. M5J 1E6
(416) 699-4666
(FAX: 416-699-5512)
Established: 1986
Membership Fee: $20 Cdn, $17 US ($2.50 Cdn, $3 US for added household member)
Includes: Membership card, bimonthly newsletter
Meetings: Monthly, on the second Saturday; special events
Current Membership: 140

USS ASTRA
433-30 AVE. N.W.,
CALGARY, ALTA. T2M 2N5
(403) 277-2237
Recognized: Chapter of Starfleet International
Established: 1990
Name: Latin for star, from club motto: "Through adversity to the stars"
Membership Fee: $1 per meeting
Includes: Newsletter, membership card
Meetings: Twice monthly, on first and third Mondays
Current Membership: 40

USS BONAVENTURE, NCC-1845
EDMONTON STAR TREK SOCIETY
P.O. BOX 11685, MAIN POST OFFICE
EDMONTON, ALTA. T6A 2J1
(403) 465-7344
Established: May 1987
Name: CHMS Bonaventure, Canada's only aircraft carrier; the USS Enterprise was also named for an aircraft carrier
Membership Fee: Adults, $15 annually; under 14, $7.50. Out of town: adults, $10; under 14, $5
Includes: Newsletter, membership card, crew handbook
Meetings: Twice monthly; six social events per year
Current Membership: 70

USS ENDEAVOUR, NCC-1991
#307-1040 PACIFIC ST.
VANCOUVER, B.C. V6E 4C1
(604) 688-6907 (FAX: 604-688-6907)
Established: September 1991
Name: Club motto, "to strive (or to endeavour) for unity"
Membership Fee: $15 annually
Includes: Membership handbook, ID card, monthly newsletter
Meetings: Monthly meetings, social and charitable events
Current Membership: 40

USS ENDEAVOUR—STARFLEET INTERNATIONAL
1509 EDMONTON ST.
PRINCE GEORGE, B.C. V2M 1X5
(604) 562-1826
Recognized: Chapter of Starfleet International
Established: 1991
Dedicated to: *ST* and science fiction
Name: The HMS Bark Endeavour, a ship captained in the late 1700s by Thomas Cook
Membership Fee: $5 per year
Includes: Membership card, officer's manual and club fanzine
Meetings: Twice monthly, first and third Wednesday; October convention
Current Membership: 20

USS EXODUS, NCC-1966
38 CALLIE RD.
HAMILTON, ONT. L9A 1Z7
(905) 387-3783
Established: March 1992
Membership Fee: $30
Includes: Newsletter
Meetings: Monthly
Current Membership: Over 50

USS HUDSON BAY—INFINITE DIVERSITY INTERNATIONAL CORPORATION
7050 WESTON RD., SUITE 301
WOODBRIDGE, ONT. L4L 8G7
(905) 850-6080 (FAX: 905-850-6082)
Established: 1990
Dedicated to: Organizing conventions and charitable events
Name: Known as the USS Hudson Bay, from the original charter for Canada grant-

ed to the Hudson Bay Group of Adventurers and Travellers
Membership Fee: $30 ($2.50 for any additional household member)
Includes: Newsletter, monthly meetings, convention organizing and charitable events
Meetings: Monthly meeting and social event
Current Membership: 200

USS KESTRAL
405B-7025 STRIDE AVE.
BURNABY, B.C. V3N 1T3
(604) 540-4909
Established: September 1982
Dedicated to: *Star Trek* movies and outdoor gaming
Name: A bird of prey; also named for Admiral Kestral
Membership Fee: $10 individual, $15 per family
Includes: Quarterly newsletter and membership card
Meetings: Social events monthly; annual Christmas party

USS OMEGA
M.P.O. BOX 1212
SAINT JOHN, N.B. E2L 4G7
(506) 672-4790
Established: 1987
Name: Federation starship
Membership Fee: $7
Includes: Bimonthly newsletter, membership handbook and card
Meetings: Twice monthly
Current Membership: 60

USS RESOLUTION
P.O. BOX 6501, DEPOT 1
VICTORIA, B.C. V8P 5M4
(604) 592-6086
Established: 1985
Name: Flagship of Capt. James Cook
Membership Fee: $18
Includes: Membership card, handbook, quarterly magazine
Meetings: Monthly; social events
Current Membership: 40

USS TERRA NOVA
R.R. #3, BOX 4-B
PORT AU PORT PENINSULA,
NFLD. A0N 1T0
Established: 1991
Name: Latin for Newfoundland
Membership Fee: $5
Includes: Twenty-Fourth Century fanzine, membership card, rank certificate
Meetings: Monthly
Current Membership: 45

USS WELFEN—GUELPH TREK CLUB
P.O. BOX 29015, EATON'S CENTRE
GUELPH, ONT. N1H 8S4
(519) 823-2224
Established: November 1990
Name: An *STNG*-type ship, set four years later; Welfen is the ancient royal family name for Guelph.
Membership Fee: $25 annually
Includes: 10 newsletters, constitution, character-generation forms
Meetings: Monthly meetings (September-June) first and third Tuesday; award nights and a charity auction
Current Membership: 30

USS YORKTOWN, c/o GREG CAMERON,
P.O. BOX 6394, STN. D
LONDON, ONT. N5W 5S4
(519) 668-0457
Established: 1992
Name: Federation starship
Membership Fee: $20
Includes: Club card, Starfleet ID card, newsletter, club certificate
Meetings: Monthly
Current Membership: 20

VULCAN ASSOCIATION FOR SCIENCE AND TREK
BOX 1701, VULCAN, ALTA. T0L 2B0
(403) 485-2633
Dedicated to: *ST*, especially Vulcans
Membership Fee: $15
Includes: Newsletter and info on Vulcan
Meetings: Monthly; July 16-17 convention
Current Membership: 36

U.S. Clubs

STAR TREK: THE OFFICIAL FAN CLUB
P.O. BOX 111000
AURORA, COLO. 80011
(303) 341-1813 (FAX: 303-341-1401)
Officially recognized: Yes
Established: 1979
Membership Fee: $14.95 US, $17 Cdn
Includes: One-year subscription to *Star Trek* magazine (a 60-page bi-monthly glossy), membership kit, catalogue
Meetings: None
Current Membership: 50,000

BEVERLYOPHILES
451-D W. SPRINGFIELD ST.
UPLAND, CA. 91786-2951
(909) 985-7791
Established: July 1989
Dedicated to: Gates McFadden
Name: Lovers of Beverly (Dr. Crusher)
Membership Fee: $30 US
Includes: 10 newsletters per year
Current Membership: 50

DATA ENTRIES
853 FALLBROOK AVE.
SAN JOSE, CA. 95130
Established: 1987
Dedicated to: Lt.-Cmdr. Data
Membership Fee: $5 US
Includes: Quarterly newsletter
Current Membership: 500

FANS OF PATRICK STEWART
P.O. BOX 7032
SAN JOSE, CA. 95150-7032
(408) 236-2127
Recognized: By Patrick Stewart
Established: August 1990
Dedicated to: Patrick Stewart and *STNG*
Membership Fee: $18 US, $20 Cdn
Includes: Quarterly newsletter, member-

ship certificate, photos, 24-hour voice mail
Current Membership: 550

INTERNATIONAL AUDIENCE ALLIANCE FOR PATRICK STEWART (IAAPS)
P.O. BOX 352
BERRYVILLE, VA. 22511
Recognized: By Patrick Stewart
Established: 1988
Dedicated to: The career of Patrick Stewart; the promotion of literacy and the arts
Membership Fee: $25 US annually
Includes: Quarterly magazine and newsletter, club directory, membership card and photo of Stewart
Meetings: At conventions and events where Patrick Stewart appears
Current Membership: 550

INTERNATIONAL FEDERATION OF TREKKERS, INC.
P.O. BOX 3123
LORAIN, OHIO
44052-7123
(216) 246-2438
Established: June 1984
Name: From United Federation of Planets
Membership Fee: $10 US; $11 US for Canadian members
Includes: IFT identification card, membership certificate, stardate chart, club newsletter
Meetings: IFT local chapter meetings
Current Membership: 2100 members worldwide in 86 chapters.

THE STAR TREK FAN CLUB OF CALIFORNIA
P.O. BOX 7094
COTATI, CA. 94931
(707) 795-6077
(FAX: 707-523-3106)
Established: October 1989
Name: Also recognized as the USS California
Membership Fee: $10 US
Includes: Monthly newsletter
Current Membership: 300

Game Solutions

TEST YOUR *NEXT GENERATION* TRIVIA (from page 50)

1. As every Trekker knows, Picard commands, "Tea. Earl Grey. Hot."

2. The USS Enterprise (NCC-1701-D) was built at the Utopia Planitia shipyard ("Eye of the Beholder," No. 270).

3. In "Timescape" (No. 251), Troi, Picard, Data and Geordi discover the Enterprise and a Romulan ship are seemingly frozen in time while firing at each other. Since the ships were trapped in a section of space bathed in bubbles that slowed time down, it was only by forcing time backward then forward that the ships escaped tragedy.

4. Rosalind Chao played Klinger's Korean war bride in *M*A*S*H*. As Keiko Ishikawa, she married Miles O'Brien ("Data's Day," No. 185). The O'Briens were reassigned to *DS9*.

5. Data's human nemesis is none other than Professor Moriarty, the archenemy of legendary detective Sherlock Holmes. In "Elementary, Dear Data" (No. 129), Moriarty (Daniel Davis) is created via the holodeck when, upon Dr. Pulaski's suggestion, Geordi orders the ship's computer to create an adversary smarter than Data. After threatening to take over the Enterprise, Moriarty's holodeck image eventually agrees to be stored in the computer until the day he can be made into matter ("Ship in a Bottle," No. 238).

6. Worf's family lost its honor when Worf's late father, Mogh, was falsely branded the traitor responsible for the Khitomer Massacre of the Klingons by the Romulans ("Sins of the Father," No. 165)—the massacre that left Worf and his younger brother, Kurn, orphans. Honor would not be regained until the two-part "Redemption" (Nos. 200, 201).

7. The Borg were stopped because they were programmed to take a nap—a weak spot in the Borg computer's basic command codes discovered by Picard ("The Best of Both Worlds II," No. 175). Data simply ordered the Borg to sleep.

8. Beth Toussaint, who played Tasha Yar's younger sister, Ishara ("Legacy," No. 180), played Tracy Lawton, the daughter of J.R.'s nemesis Carter McKay, on *Dallas*.

9. To date, Data has met his human father,

Dr. Noonian Soong ("Brothers," No. 177); his android brother, Lore ("Datalore," No. 114); and his android-but-she-doesn't-know-it mother (below), Juliana Tainer ("Inheritance," No. 262). Data also created an android daughter, Lal ("The Offspring," No. 164).

10. John de Lancie. Formerly electronic wizard Eugene Bradford on *Days of Our Lives,* de Lancie first appeared as the god-like Q in the series pilot ("Encounter at Farpoint," Nos. 101, 102) and has returned almost every season since then to infuriate Capt. Picard and his crew.

11. Alexander is Worf's son by the late Ambassador K'Ehleyr, who was murdered by Duras, a political rival ("Reunion," No. 181).

12. LeVar Burton—Geordi La Forge to Trekkers—is also host of the PBS children's program *Reading Rainbow.*

13. Beverly's late husband, Lieut. Jack Crusher, and Jean-Luc Picard served together on the USS Stargazer ("Family," No. 178). Crusher was killed when—during an Away Team emergency—Picard was forced to leave him behind to rescue another man ("Coming of Age," No. 119).

14. Data has a storage capacity of 800 quadrillion bits ("The Measure of a Man," No. 135).

15. Vash, the beautiful, scheming con artist played by Jennifer Hetrick, first appeared in "Captain's Holiday" (No. 167) and returned for another romp with Picard in "QPid" (No. 194).

16. Kelsey Grammer, better known as Dr. Frasier Crane (*Frasier, Cheers*) played Capt. Morgan Bateman of the USS Bozeman ("Cause and Effect," No. 218).

17. Although Tasha Yar (played by Denise

Crosby, Bing's granddaughter) was killed by Armus ("Skin of Evil," No. 122), Tasha remained alive in an alternate universe ("Yesterday's Enterprise," No. 163), saving the ship and returning in time with the Enterprise-C. Captured there by Romulans, she bears a daughter, Sela, and is killed trying to escape. Her daughter (also Denise Crosby) grows up to wage war for the Romulans, planning an invasion of Vulcan (two-part "Unification," Nos. 207, 208).

18. Odan the Trill and the human Riker both housed the same symbiont, who became involved with Dr. Crusher ("The Host," No. 197). When Odan's host body died and he needed a replacement, Riker served as host until the new body arrived.

19. Saul Rubinek played the infamous Kivas Fajo, a collector of rare and valuable artifacts ("The Most Toys," No. 170).

20. Jeremy Aster's mother was killed ("The Bonding," No. 153) when a bomb left over from a dead civilization's war exploded. He was eventually adopted as a brother by Worf in the R'uustai bonding ceremony.

21. David Ogden Stiers played Dr. Timicin, a scientist captivated by Lwaxana but whose culture imposes ritual suicide at age 60 ("Half a Life," No. 196).

22. Dr. Leah Brahms, who appeared via a holodeck program created by Geordi in his search for a means by which the Enterprise could escape from a Menthar energy-draining device ("Booby Trap," No. 154). Played by Susan Gibney, the real Leah proved to be rather different from her holographic image ("Galaxy's Child," No. 190).

23. After proving himself by saving Picard's life, Wesley finally leaves for Starfleet Academy ("Final Mission," No. 183). We see him again in "The Game" (No. 206), his first visit aboard the Enterprise since entering the Academy.

24. Ensign Ro Laren (played by Michelle Forbes, below with Patrick Stewart) is from the planet Bajor—a world torn apart by a lengthy war with the Cardassians. Now sit-

uated near Bajor is the Federation space station Deep Space Nine. Forbes first appeared as the Bajoran in "Ensign Ro" (No. 203).

25. In "Conspiracy" (No. 125), Lt.-Cmdr. Dexter Remmick (Robert Schenkkan) was playing host to a mother alien and her off-spring, when Picard and Riker blasted his head away, killing the aliens.

26. *Entertainment Tonight* anchor John Tesh played one of Worf's Klingon tormentors in the anniversary of his Age of Ascension rite ("The Icarus Factor," No. 140).

27. Michael Dorn—better known as Worf—played Officer Turner on *CHiPS* (1980-82).

28. Barclay (Dwight Schultz), nicknamed Lieut. Broccoli ("Hollow Pursuits," No. 169) has a sneaky habit of ducking on to the holodeck whenever life gets too stressful. There, his favorite pastime involves a fantasy where he duels with Picard and dates Troi.

29. Data became an independent being when Picard argued Data's case before a Starfleet tribunal called because cyberneticist Bruce Maddox wanted to disassemble the android to make duplicates for Starfleet ("The Measure of a Man," No. 135).

30. Bebe Neuwirth, better known as Dr. Lilith Sternin (*Cheers*), played the Malcorian nurse Lanel, whose greatest fantasy was to have sex with an alien—preferably Riker ("First Contact," No. 189).

31. Kevin Uxbridge (John Anderson), an immortal superalien disguised as a human, destroyed all 50 billion Husnock instantaneously after his wife was killed by them during his planet's invasion ("The Survivors," No. 151).

32. Lursa and B'Etor—Klingon women who wear vengeance on their sleeves and very little on their chests—are the sisters of Duras, the late contender for the Klingon throne. Their treacherous plans are revealed when they bring Duras's illegitimate son to contest Picard's decision to pass the succession of the empire to Gowron (two-part "Redemption," Nos. 200, 201).

33. None other than Jonathan Frakes, who appeared as Damon Ross on *Falcon Crest* in 1985.

34. Lwaxana Troi (Majel Barrett), of course. Deanna's mother first appeared in "Haven" (No. 105), when she tried to convince her daughter to go through with an arranged marriage. Troi has reappeared almost every season since, and drives Picard to distraction every time.

35. VISOR, the name of the device that Geordi wears to help him see, is an acronym for Visual Instrument and Sight Organ Replacement.

36. Capt. Jellico (Ronny Cox) took command when he sent the captain on a secret mission that turned into an ambush—and led to Picard's torture—by the Cardassians (two-part "Chain of Command," Nos. 236, 237).

37. As an allasomorph, or shape changer, Wesley's first love, Salia (Jaime Hubbard, below, with Wil Wheaton), possessed a flexible exoskeleton ("The Dauphin," No. 136).

38. Having injured his spine in an accident, Worf decided he'd rather die than be paralysed. He abandoned his plan to commit ritual suicide—with his son's assistance —for Alexander's sake ("Ethics," No. 216).

39. Once known as *My Favorite Martian*, Ray Walston plays Boothby, the groundskeeper at Starfleet Academy and mentor to Picard ("The First Duty," No. 219).

40. Corbin Bernsen, best known as *L.A. Law*'s Arnie Becker, turns up in the future as Q2—another representative of the Q Continuum, who suggested evicting Q for his past misdeeds ("Déjà Q," No. 161).

41. Kataan—a planet that died over a thousand years ago, and where Picard lived the life of iron weaver Kamin ("The Inner Light," No. 225).

42. Data's daughter, Lal—which means "beloved" in Hindi—was created by Data using his own neural nets. Lal (Hallie Todd) died because she couldn't handle the emotions she wasn't supposed to feel. ("The Offspring," No. 164)

43. Lieut. Aquiel Uhnari's pet dog hungers for his next victim in "Aquiel" (No. 239), until Geordi blows Fido away as he attacks.

44. Lwaxana simply wanted a traditional Betazoid wedding when she walked down the aisle in her birthday suit ("Cost of Living," No. 220). Not quite as open-minded, the groom (Tony Jay) scurried off home. His loss.

45. Jenice Manheim (Michelle Phillips), the woman Picard stood up 22 years earlier ("We'll Always Have Paris," No. 124).

46. Clara's friend, Isabella, becomes terrifyingly real when the alien—having taken human form to learn of the culture—decides that only Clara deserves to live ("Imaginary Friend," No. 222).

47. Kamala (Famke Janssen), the beautiful empathic mesomorph who accidentally bonds with Picard, is the woman bred to be a peace offering and held encased in a cocoon-like stasis field to protect her from other men ("The Perfect Mate," No. 221).

48. Stephen Hawking, renowned physicist and ardent sci-fi fan, appeared as a hologram in Data's poker game ("Descent I," No. 252).

49. Worf's foster parents are Sergey and Helena Rozhenko, originally from the farming planet Gault ("Family," No. 178).

50. The Enterprise has 42 decks—with the main bridge of the saucer section the first, and subsequent decks numbered downward from there.

TEST YOUR KLINGON (from page 48)

Mystery Klingon phrases:
bIjeghbe' chugh vaj bIHegh ("Surrender or die!"); **bortaS bIr jablu' DI' reH QaQqu' nay'** ("Revenge is a dish which is best served cold"); **Duj tlvoqtaH** ("Always trust your instincts"); **pItlh** (I've done it!"); **DaH yIDII** ("Pay now!"); **nuqneH** ("What do you want?") and **batlh Daqawlu'taH** ("You will be remembered with honor").

[Note: The unused letters falling in sequence, from the top left-hand corner to the bottom right, were used to make up these phrases.]

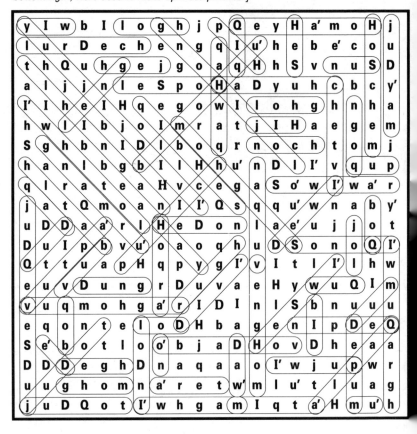